I0109635

Dedications

This book is dedicated to Matt Osborne, former deputy legal counsel at the North Carolina Administrative Office of the Courts. Matt created a table of license revocations and their corresponding limited privileges that I have relied on for years. That now dog-eared document was the inspiration for this expanded work. Matt himself is an inspiration, embodying the best of a dedicated public servant and brilliant lawyer and being a good friend to boot. The book is also dedicated to Kevin Justice, director of academic publications at the School of Government. This publication was an impossible-to-read Excel spreadsheet before Kevin made sense of it and put it in a format that others could read. Thank you, Kevin, for working your magic and for patiently ushering this work into existence.

Contents

Alcohol, Drugs, and Impairment

Introduction

[*Author's Note:* This publication has been updated to include legislative changes from S.L. 2025-71, applicable to offenses committed on or after December 1, 2025.]

The North Carolina Division of Motor Vehicles (NC DMV), a Division within the State's Department of Transportation, has the exclusive power to issue, suspend, or revoke a person's North Carolina driver's license.[1] There are more than 8 million licensed drivers in North Carolina, and there are more than 1 million people whose licenses have been revoked by NC DMV.[2] A small number of those people (around 6,000) have been issued a limited driving privilege by the courts that authorizes driving during the period of revocation, subject to certain limitations.

A person whose license has been revoked by NC DMV may have the license reinstated at the end of the revocation period, but in certain circumstances, restrictions are placed on the reinstated license. More than 100,000 drivers licensed by NC DMV have alcohol restrictions on their licenses, and more than 30,000 are permitted to drive only a vehicle equipped with an ignition interlock device, which permits a vehicle's engine to engage only after a person has submitted a breath sample that registers below the programmed alcohol concentration limit.

This publication lists triggering events and convictions that may result in the revocation of a person's driver's license, the length of that revocation, whether a limited driving privilege may issue and the limitations of any such privilege, and the mandatory conditions that apply when the person's license is restored.

---

1. Joyner v. Garrett, 279 N.C. 226, 232 (1971) ("The power to issue, suspend, or revoke a driver's license is vested exclusively in the Department of Motor Vehicles, subject to review by the Superior Court and, upon appeal, by the appellate division."). The term "license" includes any driver's license or permit to operate a motor vehicle including (a) any temporary license or permit, (b) the privilege of any person to drive a motor vehicle regardless of whether the person has a valid license, and (c) any nonresident's operating privilege. Chapter 20, Section 4.01(17) of the North Carolina General Statutes (hereinafter G.S.).

2. The numbers reported in this section are based on the results of data control results retrieved by NC DMV on February 5, 2024.

Triggering Event or Conviction

Conviction-Based License Revocations

When a person is convicted of certain criminal offenses, NC DMV is authorized—and is sometimes required—to revoke the offender's driver's license (which includes any operating privilege)[3] for a specified period of time.

The term "conviction" includes a conviction for an offense committed in North Carolina or another state.[4] When referring to an offense committed in North Carolina, the term "conviction" means any of the following:

- a final conviction[5] of a criminal offense, including a no contest plea;
- a determination that a person is responsible for an infraction, including a no contest plea;
- an unvacated forfeiture of cash in the full amount of a bond required by Article 26 of Chapter 15A of the General Statutes;
- a third or subsequent prayer for judgment continued within any five-year period; or
- any prayer for judgment continued if the offender holds a commercial drivers license or if the offense occurs in a commercial motor vehicle.

Out-of-State Convictions

When referring to an offense committed outside North Carolina, the term "conviction" means any of the following:

- an unvacated adjudication of guilt;
- a determination that a person has violated or failed to comply with the law in a court of original jurisdiction or an authorized administrative tribunal;
- an unvacated forfeiture of bail or collateral deposited to secure the person's appearance in court;
- a violation of a condition of release without bail, regardless of whether or not the penalty is rebated, suspended, or probated;
- a final conviction of a criminal offense, including a no contest plea; or
- any prayer for judgment continued, including any payment of a fine or court costs, if the offender holds a commercial driver's license or if the offense occurs in a commercial motor vehicle.

---

3. In any case in which NC DMV is authorized to revoke the license of a person who does not have a license, DMV may revoke the operating privilege of the person in the same manner as if such person held a driver's license. G.S. 20-23.1.

4. G.S. 4-01(4a). The term "state" is defined to include a "state, territory, or possession of the United States, District of Columbia, Commonwealth of Puerto Rico, a province of Canada, or the Sovereign Nation of the Eastern Band of the Cherokee Indians with tribal lands, as defined in 18 U.S.C. § 1151, located within the boundaries of the State of North Carolina." G.S. 20-4.01(45) (further providing that for provisions of G.S. Chapter 20 that apply to commercial driver's licenses, "'state' means a state of the United States and the District of Columbia").

5. A "final conviction" is an adjudication of guilt plus the entry of a judgment from which a defendant can exercise his or her right to appeal. *See* Barbour v. Scheidt, 246 N.C. 169, 173 (1957). NC DMV is not authorized to revoke a driver's license based on a conviction that is pending appeal. G.S. 20-16(b).

NC DMV is authorized to revoke the license of any North Carolina resident upon receiving notice of the person's conviction in another state of any of the following offenses:

- exceeding a stated speed limit of 55 miles per hour or more by more than 15 miles per hour,
- driving while the person's license is suspended or revoked,
- careless and reckless driving,
- engaging in prearranged speed competition,
- engaging willfully in speed competition,
- hit-and-run driving resulting in damage to property,
- unlawfully passing a stopped school bus,
- illegal transportation of alcoholic beverages, and
- any of the offenses included in G.S. 20-17 that require mandatory license revocation.[6]

---

6. G.S. 20-23 (stating that NC DMV may revoke for any of the offenses listed in G.S.20-26(a), which lists the out-of-state convictions for which NC DMV must keep records; G.S. 20-26(a) includes the offenses in G.S. 20-17). The offenses listed in G.S. 20-17 that require revocation are as follows:

- manslaughter (or negligent homicide) resulting from the operation of a motor vehicle;
- impaired driving under G.S. 20-138.1;
- impaired driving under G.S. 20-138.2, if the driver's alcohol concentration level was .06 or higher;
- any felony in the commission of which a motor vehicle is used;
- failure to stop and render aid in violation of G.S. 20-166(a) or (b);
- perjury or the making of a false affidavit or statement under oath to NC DMV;
- conviction, within a period of twelve months, of (1) two charges of reckless driving, (2) two charges of aggressive driving, or (3) one or more charges of reckless driving and one or more charges of aggressive driving;
- conviction upon one charge of aggressive driving or reckless driving while engaged in the illegal transportation of intoxicants for the purpose of sale;
- conviction of using a false or fictitious name or giving a false or fictitious address in an application for a driver's license; knowingly making a false statement or concealing a material fact or otherwise committing a fraud in any such application; or procuring or knowingly permitting another to commit any of the foregoing acts;
- any offense set forth under G.S. 20-141.4;
- conviction of assault with a motor vehicle;
- a second or subsequent conviction of transporting an open container of alcoholic beverage under G.S. 20-138.7;
- a second or subsequent conviction, as defined in G.S. 20-138.2A(d), of driving a commercial motor vehicle after consuming alcohol under G.S. 20-138.2A;
- a conviction of driving a school bus, school activity bus, or child care vehicle after consuming alcohol under G.S. 20-138.2B;
- a conviction of malicious use of an explosive or incendiary device to damage property (G.S. 14-49(b) and (b1)); making a false report concerning a destructive device in a public building (G.S. 14-69.1(c)); perpetrating a hoax concerning a destructive device in a public building (G.S. 14-69.2(c)); possessing or carrying a dynamite cartridge, bomb, grenade, mine, or powerful explosive on educational property (G.S. 14-269.2(b1)); or causing, encouraging, or aiding a minor to possess or carry a dynamite cartridge, bomb, grenade, mine, or powerful explosive on educational property (G.S. 14-269.2(c1));
- a second or subsequent conviction of larceny of motor fuel under G.S. 14-72.5; and
- a third or subsequent conviction of operating a private passenger automobile with prohibited modifications on any highway or public vehicular area under G.S. 20-135.4(d).

G.S. 20-26(a) also requires NC DMV to keep a record of any conviction occurring outside of North Carolina for any serious traffic violation that involves a commercial motor vehicle and is not otherwise required to be kept. Thus, NC DMV presumably may revoke a person's driver's license for conviction of such an offense.

NC DMV is authorized to revoke a person's driver's license for a conviction in federal court of an offense involving impaired driving just as if the person had been convicted in a North Carolina court.[7] A nonresident's privilege to drive a motor vehicle in North Carolina is subject to revocation for the same reasons and in the same manner as a North Carolina driver's license.[8]

The table that follows includes entries for out-of-state or federal convictions when those convictions result in revocations for which a limited driving privilege may be applied for and which may be issued on different terms and/or using different forms than apply to an in-state conviction.

Convictions More than Ten Years Old Generally Not Considered

In general, NC DMV may not consider a conviction for a violation of the motor vehicle laws that occurred more than ten years in the past.[9] Exceptions apply for the following offenses:

- offenses occurring in a commercial motor vehicle and
- offenses by the holder of a commercial drivers license involving a noncommercial motor vehicle.[10]

Offenses for which a conviction triggers a license revocation are listed in the first two columns of the following table. When a person is convicted of violating a law regulating the operation of a vehicle or an offense for which NC DMV is authorized or required to revoke the person's driver's license, the clerk of superior court must notify NC DMV of the conviction.[11] When this occurs, NC DMV then notifies the person that the revocation becomes effective at 12:01 a.m. on the eleventh day after notification. This ten-day notice period is not explicitly required by statute but corresponds to the ten-day period for filing a notice of appeal to superior court for trial de novo, thus ensuring that NC DMV does not impose a collateral licensure consequence for a district court conviction that is not yet final.

Other Conduct Leading to Revocation

NC DMV also may revoke a person's driver's license for other types of conduct such as willfully refusing to submit to testing pursuant to the state's implied consent laws, being charged with an implied consent offense and registering a threshold alcohol concentration, or failing to appear in court for or to pay a fine associated with a motor vehicle offense. Certain types of conduct short of a criminal conviction that can trigger license revocation are listed by description in the table, following the list of convictions that trigger revocation.

---

7. G.S. 20-23.2.
8. G.S. 20-22.
9. G.S. 20-36.
10. An exception to the ten-year look-back rule also applies to a second failure to submit to a chemical test when charged with an implied-consent offense, as defined in G.S. 20-16.2, that occurred while the person was driving a commercial motor vehicle. G.S. 20-36.
11. G.S. 20-24(b).

Limited Driving Privileges

Even though NC DMV is the state's exclusive licensing authority, a court may in certain instances grant a limited driving privilege authorizing driving by a person whose license is revoked. A limited driving privilege is a court order that permits a person with a revoked driver's license to drive subject to any additional limitations required by law or imposed in the court's discretion. To be eligible for a limited driving privilege, a person must petition the court for the issuance of the privilege, satisfy eligibility requirements defined by statute, and demonstrate good cause for the issuance of the privilege. The person must also pay a $100 processing fee to the clerk of superior court in the county in which the limited driving privilege is issued.[12] Thus, a limited driving privilege is a judgment issued in the discretion of the court authorizing a person to drive, often for limited purposes and at prescribed times, during the period of revocation.

Copies of all limited driving privileges that are issued by a court must be sent to NC DMV.[13] If NC DMV receives a privilege that is invalid on its face (meaning that it is not authorized by statute or does not contain required limitations), the agency must immediately notify the court and the holder of the privilege that it considers the privilege void and that NC DMV records will not indicate that the holder has a limited driving privilege.[14]

The table specifies whether, for each type of revocation, a limited driving privilege may be issued, the eligibility requirements for the privilege, the permissible duration of the privilege, the judicial official who may issue the privilege, the statute that governs the terms of the privilege, what restrictions the privilege must contain, and any applicable forms.

There are two primary types of limited driving privileges—those issued pursuant to G.S. 20-16.1 and those issued pursuant to 20-179.3. The first type permits but does not require the court to impose restrictions on times, vehicles, routes, and purposes of driving. These privileges are primarily, though not exclusively, authorized to allow driving during a revocation resulting from a speeding-related offense. The second type permits essential driving for limited purposes and at limited times as provided by statute. These privileges are primarily, though not exclusively, authorized to allow driving during a revocation resulting from an impairment or alcohol-related driving offense. The time and purpose restrictions associated with the second type of privilege do not apply if an ignition interlock restriction (discussed below) is imposed.

License Restoration

A person whose license has been revoked may apply for his or her license to be restored at the conclusion of a statutory revocation period. A person who seeks to have his or her license restored following a revocation must pay a restoration fee as specified by statute.[15] Before NC DMV may restore a driver's license revoked under any provision of Chapter 20 other than G.S. 20-24.1, the person must submit proof of financial responsibility or proof that financial responsibility is not required because the person (a) does not own currently registered motor

---

12. G.S. 20-20.2.
13. G.S. 20-179.3(k).
14. *Id.*
15. *See* G.S. 20-7(i1).

vehicles and (b) does not operate nonfleet private passenger vehicles that are owned by other persons and that are not insured under commercial motor vehicle liability insurance policies.[16]

Alcohol Concentration Restrictions

Licenses that are restored following a revocation for conviction of an alcohol-related driving offense are restored with a restriction that prohibits the person from driving with an alcohol concentration of 0.04, 0.02, or 0.00 at any relevant time after the driving.[17] In most cases, the restriction remains in effect for three years.[18]

A person seeking restoration of a license that will be restored with an alcohol concentration restriction must agree to submit to a chemical analysis (that is a test of the person's breath, blood, or other bodily fluid) under the state's implied consent laws when certain conditions are met.[19] Thus, the person must agree to submit to testing at the request of a law enforcement officer who has reasonable grounds to believe the person is operating a motor vehicle on a highway or public vehicular area (1) while consuming alcohol or (2) at any time while the person has remaining in his or her body any alcohol or controlled substance previously consumed. The person also must agree that upon a law enforcement officer's request, the person will agree to be transported by the law enforcement officer to the place where the chemical analysis will be administered.

Ignition Interlock Restrictions

A person whose license is revoked for a conviction of impaired driving under G.S. 20-138.1 or habitual impaired driving under G.S. 20-138.5 will, in certain circumstances, be limited to driving only a vehicle equipped with an ignition interlock device (IID) upon the restoration of his or her license. An IID is attached to a vehicle and permits the vehicle's engine to engage only after a person has submitted a breath sample that registers below the programmed alcohol concentration limit. An IID thereafter requires intermittent testing while the vehicle is in operation and an arrival test before the vehicle's ignition is switched off. An ignition interlock requirement applies when any of the following conditions are met: (1) the person had an alcohol concentration of 0.15 or more; (2) the person has been convicted of another offense involving impaired driving that occurred within seven years of the date of the offense for which the person's license has been revoked; (3) the person was sentenced at Aggravated Level One for the underlying offense of impaired driving; or (4) the person's license was revoked as a result of a conviction of habitual impaired driving.[20] Beginning December 1, 2024, driver's licenses revoked for conviction of any of the felony death or serious injury offenses set out in G.S. 20-141.4 also are subject to an IID restriction upon restoration.[21] When such a person's license is restored, NC DMV will impose the following restrictions: the person can operate a vehicle only if (1) it is equipped with an approved IID, (2) the person personally activates the IID before driving,

---

16. G.S. 20-19(k).
17. G.S. 20-19(c3).
18. *Id.*
19. *Id.*
20. G.S. 20-17.8(a), (a1).
21. S.L. 2024-43, § 2.(b) (effective December 1, 2024, for driver's licenses revoked on or after that date).

and (3) the person does not drive with an alcohol concentration of 0.02 or greater.[22] A person subject to an ignition interlock restriction must identify any registered vehicle or vehicles that he or she owns and operates or intends to operate and have the designated vehicle(s) equipped with ignition interlock.[23] The person must present proof that an IID has been installed in at least one designated vehicle of those that the person owns before NC DMV may issue a license to the person.[24] The requirements remain in effect for one year from the date of restoration if the original revocation period was one year, three years from the date of restoration if the period was four years, and seven years from the date of revocation if the revocation was permanent.[25]

The table sets forth the license restorations to which an IID restriction applies. It also sets forth the types of limited driving privileges for which ignition interlock is required.[26] If the person was eligible for and received a limited driving privilege under G.S. 20-179.3 that required ignition interlock, the period of time for which that limited driving privilege was held must be applied towards the duration requirements of subsection G.S. 20-17.8(c).[27]

Conditional Restoration

Several types of revocations are designated by statute as having a permanent duration. Notwithstanding their designation as "permanent," NC DMV may conditionally restore some types of permanently revoked licenses. In addition, NC DMV is authorized to conditionally restore licenses revoked both permanently and for shorter periods for certain enumerated offenses. The table reflects the convictions leading to revocation for which a conditional restoration is authorized, the controlling statute, eligibility requirements, and applicable restrictions.

---

22. G.S. 20-17.8(b).
23. G.S. 20-17.8(c1).
24. *Id.*
25. G.S. 20-17.8(c).
26. *See* G.S. 20-179.3(g3), (g5).
27. G.S. 20-17.8(d).

Reckless Driving and Speeding

Conviction Statute	Offense Description / Triggering Event	Revocation Statute	Length of Revocation; Statute
G.S. 20-140; G.S. 20-141	**Conviction within 12 months of 1 or more charges of reckless driving and 1 or more charges of speeding in excess of 55 m.p.h. and not more than 80 m.p.h.**	Discretionary revocation: G.S. 20-16(a)(9)	≤ 6 months; G.S. 20-19(a)
	Limited driving privilege authorized: G.S. 20-16(e1).		
	Eligibility requirements: No convictions of any other moving violation within past 12 months. *Duration:* Authorized for up to 12 months. *Issuing official:* Trial judge. *Statutory terms:* G.S. 20-16.1(b). *Restrictions:* Any restrictions the court deems advisable. Can include conditions of days, hours, types of vehicles, routes, geographical boundaries, and specific purposes for which limited driving privilege is allowed. Person must provide proof of financial responsibility and must maintain financial responsibility during the term of the limited driving privilege (or must sign a written certificate indicating that the person (1) does not own a registered vehicle and (2) does not operate any nonfleet private passenger vehicle owned by another that is not covered by commercial-auto liability insurance). *Forms:* AOC-CR-306.		
	Out-of-state conviction leading to conviction within 12 months of 1 or more charges of reckless driving and 1 or more charges of speeding in excess of 55 m.p.h. and not more than 80 m.p.h.	Discretionary revocation: G.S. 20-16(a)(9)	≤ 6 months; G.S. 20-19(a)
	Limited driving privilege authorized: G.S. 20-16(e1).		
	Eligibility requirements: No convictions of any other moving violation within past 12 months. *Duration:* Authorized for up to 12 months. *Issuing official:* District court judge of the district where petitioner lives. *Statutory terms:* G.S. 20-16.1(b). *Restrictions:* Any restrictions the court deems advisable. Can include conditions of days, hours, types of vehicles, routes, geographical boundaries, and specific purposes for which limited driving privilege is allowed. Person must provide proof of financial responsibility and must maintain financial responsibility during the term of the limited driving privilege (or must sign a written certificate indicating that the person (1) does not own a registered vehicle and (2) does not operate any nonfleet private passenger vehicle owned by another that is not covered by commercial-auto liability insurance). *Forms:* AOC-CV-350 (petition); AOC-CV-351 (privilege).		
G.S. 20-140 (reckless driving); G.S. 20-141.6 (aggressive driving)	**Conviction of 1 charge of aggressive driving or reckless driving while engaged in illegal transportation of intoxicants for sale**	G.S. 20-17(a)(7)	1 year; G.S. 20-19(f)
G.S. 20-140; G.S. 20-141.6	**Conviction within 12 months of (a) 2 charges of reckless driving, (b) 2 charges of aggressive driving, or (c) a charge of reckless driving and a charge of aggressive driving**	G.S. 20-17(a)(6)	1 year; G.S. 20-19(f)
G.S. 20-141	**Conviction within 12 months of 2 or more charges of speeding more than 55 m.p.h. and not more than 80 m.p.h.**	Discretionary revocation: G.S. 20-16(a)(9)	≤ 6 months; G.S. 20-19(a)
	Limited driving privilege authorized: G.S. 20-16(e1).		
	Eligibility requirements: No convictions of any other moving violation within past 12 months. *Duration:* Authorized for up to 12 months. *Issuing official:* Trial judge. *Statutory terms:* G.S. 20-16.1(b). *Restrictions:* Any restrictions the court deems advisable. Can include conditions of days, hours, types of vehicles, routes, geographical boundaries, and specific purposes for which limited driving privilege is allowed. Person must provide proof of financial responsibility and must maintain financial responsibility during the term of the limited driving privilege (or must sign a written certificate indicating that the person (1) does not own a registered vehicle and (2) does not operate any nonfleet private passenger vehicle owned by another that is not covered by commercial-auto liability insurance). *Forms:* AOC-CR-306.		

Reckless Driving and Speeding *(continued)*

Conviction Statute	Offense Description / Triggering Event	Revocation Statute	Length of Revocation; Statute
	Out-of-state conviction of exceeding stated speed limit of 55 m.p.h. by more than 15 m.p.h. leading to conviction within 12 months of 2 or more charges of speeding more than 55 m.p.h. and not more than 80 m.p.h.	Discretionary revocation: G.S. 20-16(a)(9)	≤ 6 months; G.S. 20-19(a)

Limited driving privilege authorized: G.S. 20-16(e1).

Eligibility requirements: No convictions of any other moving violation within past 12 months.

Duration: Authorized for up to 12 months.

Issuing official: District court judge of the district where petitioner lives.

Statutory terms: G.S. 20-16.1(b).

Restrictions: Any restrictions the court deems advisable. Can include conditions of days, hours, types of vehicles, routes, geographical boundaries, and specific purposes for which limited driving privilege is allowed. Person must provide proof of financial responsibility and must maintain financial responsibility during the term of the limited driving privilege (or must sign a written certificate indicating that the person (1) does not own a registered vehicle and (2) does not operate any nonfleet private passenger vehicle owned by another that is not covered by commercial-auto liability insurance).

Forms: AOC-CV-350 (petition); AOC-CV-351 (privilege).

| G.S. 20-141 | **Speeding (a) over 15 m.p.h. over limit and over 55 m.p.h. (includes work-zone charges) or (b) over 80 m.p.h.** | G.S. 20-16.1 | First offense: 30-day suspension; second offense: 60-day suspension; G.S. 20-16.1(a), (c) |

Limited driving privilege authorized: G.S. 20-16.1(b)(1).

Eligibility requirements: No conviction for prior offense under G.S. 20-16.1(a). No prior offense occurring more than 7 years before date of current offense may be considered. Proof of financial responsibility. G.S. 20-16.1(g).

Duration: Valid for 30 days.

Issuing official: Trial judge.

Statutory terms: G.S. 20-16.1(b).

Restrictions: Any restrictions the court deems advisable. Can include conditions of days, hours, types of vehicles, routes, geographical boundaries, and specific purposes for which limited driving privilege is allowed. Person must provide proof of financial responsibility and must maintain financial responsibility during the term of the limited driving privilege (or must sign a written certificate indicating that the person (1) does not own a registered vehicle and (2) does not operate any nonfleet private passenger vehicle owned by another that is not covered by commercial-auto liability insurance).

Forms: AOC-CR-306.

| | **Out-of-state conviction for speeding over 15 m.p.h. over limit and over 55 m.p.h.** | G.S. 20-16.1 | First offense: 30-day suspension; second offense: 60-day suspension; G.S. 20-16.1(a), (c) |

Limited driving privilege authorized: G.S. 20-16.1(b)(3).

Eligibility requirements: No conviction for prior offense under G.S. 20-16.1(a). No prior offense occurring more than 7 years before date of current offense may be considered. Proof of financial responsibility required. G.S. 20-16.1(g).

Duration: Valid for 30 days.

Issuing official: District court judge of the district where petitioner lives.

Statutory terms: G.S. 20-16.1(b).

Restrictions: Any restrictions the court deems advisable. Can include conditions of days, hours, types of vehicles, routes, geographical boundaries, and specific purposes for which limited driving privilege is allowed. Person must provide proof of financial responsibility and must maintain financial responsibility during the term of the limited driving privilege (or must sign a written certificate indicating that the person (1) does not own a registered vehicle and (2) does not operate any nonfleet private passenger vehicle owned by another that is not covered by commercial-auto liability insurance).

Forms: AOC-CV-350 (petition); AOC-CV-351 (privilege).

Reckless Driving and Speeding *(continued)*

Conviction Statute	Offense Description / Triggering Event	Revocation Statute	Length of Revocation; Statute
G.S. 20-141	**Speeding (a) over 15 m.p.h. over limit and over 55 m.p.h. (includes work-zone charges) or (b) over 80 m.p.h., while, on the same occasion, violating the laws against reckless driving**	G.S. 20-16.1	60-day suspension; G.S. 20-16.1(d)

Limited driving privilege authorized: G.S. 20-16.1(b)(1).

Eligibility requirements: No conviction for prior offense under G.S. 20-16.1(a). No prior offense occurring more than 7 years before date of current offense may be considered.

Duration: Valid for 30 days.

Issuing official: Trial judge.

Statutory terms: G.S. 20-16.1(b).

Restrictions: Any restrictions the court deems advisable. Can include conditions of days, hours, types of vehicles, routes, geographical boundaries, and specific purposes for which limited driving privilege is allowed. Person must provide proof of financial responsibility and must maintain financial responsibility during the term of the limited driving privilege (or must sign a written certificate indicating that the person (1) does not own a registered vehicle and (2) does not operate any nonfleet private passenger vehicle owned by another that is not covered by commercial-auto liability insurance).

Forms: AOC-CR-306.

	Offense Description / Triggering Event	Revocation Statute	Length of Revocation; Statute
	Out-of-state conviction leading to conviction for speeding (a) over 15 m.p.h. over limit and over 55 m.p.h. or (b) over 80 m.p.h. while, on the same occasion, violating the laws against reckless driving	G.S. 20-16.1	60-day suspension; G.S. 20-16.1(d)

Limited driving privilege authorized: G.S. 20-16.1(b)(3).

Eligibility requirements: No conviction for prior offense under G.S. 20-16.1(a). No prior offense occurring more than 7 years before date of current offense may be considered.

Duration: Valid for 30 days.

Issuing official: District court judge of the district where petitioner lives.

Statutory terms: G.S. 20-16.1(b).

Restrictions: Any restrictions the court deems advisable. Can include conditions of days, hours, types of vehicles, routes, geographical boundaries, and specific purposes for which limited driving privilege is allowed. Person must provide proof of financial responsibility and must maintain financial responsibility during the term of the limited driving privilege (or must sign a written certificate indicating that the person (1) does not own a registered vehicle and (2) does not operate any nonfleet private passenger vehicle owned by another that is not covered by commercial-auto liability insurance).

Forms: AOC-CV-350 (petition); AOC-CV-351 (privilege).

Conviction Statute	Offense Description / Triggering Event	Revocation Statute	Length of Revocation; Statute
G.S. 20-141	**Conviction of speeding more than 75 m.p.h. where speed limit is less than 70 m.p.h.**	Discretionary revocation: G.S. 20-16(a)(10)	≤ 12 months; G.S. 20-19(b)

Limited driving privilege authorized: G.S. 20-16(e1).

Eligibility requirements: No convictions of any other moving violation within past 12 months.

Duration: Authorized for up to 12 months.

Issuing official: Trial judge.

Statutory terms: G.S. 20-16.1(b).

Restrictions: Any restrictions the court deems advisable. Can include conditions of days, hours, types of vehicles, routes, geographical boundaries, and specific purposes for which limited driving privilege is allowed. Person must provide proof of financial responsibility and must maintain financial responsibility during the term of the limited driving privilege (or must sign a written certificate indicating that the person (1) does not own a registered vehicle and (2) does not operate any nonfleet private passenger vehicle owned by another that is not covered by commercial-auto liability insurance).

Forms: AOC-CR-306.

Reckless Driving and Speeding *(continued)*

Conviction Statute	Offense Description / Triggering Event	Revocation Statute	Length of Revocation; Statute
G.S. 20-141	**Conviction of speeding more than 80 m.p.h. where speed limit is 70 m.p.h.**	Discretionary revocation: G.S. 20-16(a)(10a)	≤ 1 year; G.S. 20-19(c)
	Limited driving privilege authorized: G.S. 20-16(e1).		
	Eligibility requirements: No convictions of any other moving violation within past 12 months.		
	Duration: Authorized for up to 12 months.		
	Issuing official: Trial judge.		
	Statutory terms: G.S. 20-16.1(b).		
	Restrictions: Any restrictions the court deems advisable. Can include conditions of days, hours, types of vehicles, routes, geographical boundaries, and specific purposes for which limited driving privilege is allowed. Person must provide proof of financial responsibility and must maintain financial responsibility during the term of the limited driving privilege (or must sign a written certificate indicating that the person (1) does not own a registered vehicle and (2) does not operate any nonfleet private passenger vehicle owned by another that is not covered by commercial-auto liability insurance).		
	Forms: AOC-CR-306.		
G.S. 20-141; G.S. 20-141.6	**Conviction within 12 months of 1 or more charges of aggressive driving and 1 or more charges of speeding in excess of 55 m.p.h. and not more than 80 m.p.h.**	Discretionary revocation: G.S. 20-16(a)(9)	≤ 6 months; G.S. 20-19(a)
	Limited driving privilege authorized: G.S. 20-16(e1).		
	Eligibility requirements: No convictions of any other moving violation within past 12 months.		
	Duration: Authorized for up to 12 months.		
	Issuing official: Trial judge.		
	Statutory terms: G.S. 20-16.1(b).		
	Restrictions: Any restrictions the court deems advisable. Can include conditions of days, hours, types of vehicles, routes, geographical boundaries, and specific purposes for which limited driving privilege is allowed. Person must provide proof of financial responsibility and must maintain financial responsibility during the term of the limited driving privilege (or must sign a written certificate indicating that the person (1) does not own a registered vehicle and (2) does not operate any nonfleet private passenger vehicle owned by another that is not covered by commercial-auto liability insurance).		
	Forms: AOC-CR-306.		
	Out-of-state conviction leading to conviction within 12 months of 1 or more charges of aggressive driving and 1 or more charges of speeding in excess of 55 m.p.h. and not more than 80 m.p.h.	Discretionary revocation: G.S. 20-16(a)(9)	≤ 6 months; G.S. 20-19(a)
	Limited driving privilege authorized: G.S. 20-16(e1).		
	Eligibility requirements: No convictions of any other moving violation within past 12 months.		
	Duration: Authorized for up to 12 months.		
	Issuing official: District court judge of the district where petitioner lives.		
	Statutory terms: G.S. 20-16.1(b).		
	Restrictions: Any restrictions the court deems advisable. Can include conditions of days, hours, types of vehicles, routes, geographical boundaries, and specific purposes for which limited driving privilege is allowed. Person must provide proof of financial responsibility and must maintain financial responsibility during the term of the limited driving privilege (or must sign a written certificate indicating that the person (1) does not own a registered vehicle and (2) does not operate any nonfleet private passenger vehicle owned by another that is not covered by commercial-auto liability insurance).		
	Forms: AOC-CV-350 (petition); AOC-CV-351 (privilege).		
G.S. 20-141.3(a)	**Engaging in a prearranged speed competition with another motor vehicle (offenses committed before Dec. 1, 2025)**	G.S. 20-141.3(d)	3 years; G.S. 20-141.3(d)
	Conditional restoration authorized: G.S. 20-141.3(d).		
	After this time period of revocation: 18 months.		
	Eligibility requirements: Satisfactory proof that the person has been of good behavior for the past 18 months and that the person's conduct and attitude entitle the person to favorable consideration.		
	Restrictions: NC DMV may impose terms and conditions for the remainder of the original revocation period.		

Reckless Driving and Speeding *(continued)*

Conviction Statute	Offense Description / Triggering Event	Revocation Statute	Length of Revocation; Statute
G.S. 20-141.3(a)	**Engaging in a prearranged speed competition with another motor vehicle (offenses committed on or after Dec. 1, 2025)**	G.S. 20-141.3(d)(3)	3 years; G.S. 20-141.3(d)(3)
	Conditional restoration authorized: G.S. 20-141.3(d)(3), (d1).		
	After this time period of revocation: 18 months. *Eligibility requirements:* Satisfactory proof that the person has been of good behavior during the revocation period and that the person's conduct and attitude entitle the person to favorable consideration. *Restrictions:* NC DMV may impose terms and conditions for the remainder of the original revocation period.		
G.S. 20-141.3(a), (c2)	**Engaging in a prearranged speed competition with another motor vehicle causing serious injury (offenses committed on or after Dec. 1, 2025)**	G.S. 20-141.3(d)(1)	4 years; G.S. 20-141.3(d)(1)
	Conditional restoration authorized: G.S. 20-141.3(d)(1), (d1).		
	After this time period of revocation: 3 years. *Eligibility requirements:* Satisfactory proof that the person has been of good behavior during the revocation period and that the person's conduct and attitude entitle the person to favorable consideration. *Restrictions:* NC DMV may impose terms and conditions for the remainder of the original revocation period.		
G.S. 20-141.3(a), (c3)	**Engaging in a prearranged speed competition with another motor vehicle causing serious bodily injury or death (offenses committed on or after Dec. 1, 2025)**	G.S. 20-141.3(d)(2)	Permanent; G.S. 20-141.3(d)(2)
	Conditional restoration authorized: G.S. 20-141.3(d)(2), (d1).		
	After this time period of revocation: 7 years. *Eligibility requirements:* Satisfactory proof that the person has been of good behavior during the revocation period and that the person's conduct and attitude entitle the person to favorable consideration. *Restrictions:* NC DMV may impose terms and conditions for the remainder of the original revocation period.		
G.S. 20-141.3(b)	**Willfully engaging in a speed competition with another motor vehicle (not prearranged)**	Discretionary revocation: G.S. 20-141.3(e)	≤ 1 year; G.S. 20-141.3(e)
G.S. 20-141.3(c)	**Placing or receiving a bet or wager on a prearranged speed competition (offenses committed before Dec. 1, 2025)**	G.S. 20-141.3(d)	3 years; G.S. 20-141.3(d)
	Conditional restoration authorized: G.S. 20-141.3(d).		
	After this time period of revocation: 18 months. *Eligibility requirements:* Satisfactory proof that the person has been of good behavior for the past 18 months and that the person's conduct and attitude entitle the person to favorable consideration. *Restrictions:* NC DMV may impose terms and conditions for the remainder of the original revocation period.		
G.S. 20-141.3(c)	**Allowing or authorizing others to use one's motor vehicle in a prearranged speed competition (offenses committed before Dec. 1, 2025)**	G.S. 20-141.3(d)	3 years; G.S. 20-141.3(d)
	Conditional restoration authorized: G.S. 20-141.3(d).		
	After this time period of revocation: 18 months. *Eligibility requirements:* Satisfactory proof that the person has been of good behavior for the past 18 months and that the person's conduct and attitude entitle the person to favorable consideration. *Restrictions:* NC DMV may impose terms and conditions for the remainder of the original revocation period.		
G.S. 20-141.3(c)	**Allowing or authorizing others to use one's motor vehicle in a prearranged speed competition (offenses committed on or after Dec. 1, 2025)**	G.S. 20-141.3(d)(3)	3 years; G.S. 20-141.3(d)(3)
	Conditional restoration authorized: G.S. 20-141.3(d)(1), (d1).		
	After this time period of revocation: 18 months. *Eligibility requirements:* Satisfactory proof that the person has been of good behavior during the revocation period and that the person's conduct and attitude entitle the person to favorable consideration. *Restrictions:* NC DMV may impose terms and conditions for the remainder of the original revocation period.		

Reckless Driving and Speeding *(continued)*

Conviction Statute	Offense Description / Triggering Event	Revocation Statute	Length of Revocation; Statute
G.S. 20-141.3(c), (c2)	**Allowing or authorizing others to use one's motor vehicle in a prearranged speed competition causing serious injury (offenses committed on or after Dec. 1, 2025)**	G.S. 20-141.3(d)(1)	4 years; G.S. 20-141.3(d)(1)
	Conditional restoration authorized: G.S. 20-141.3(d)(1), (d1).		
	After this time period of revocation: 3 years. *Eligibility requirements:* Satisfactory proof that the person has been of good behavior during the revocation period and that the person's conduct and attitude entitle the person to favorable consideration. *Restrictions:* NC DMV may impose terms and conditions for the remainder of the original revocation period.		
G.S. 20-141.3(c), (c3)	**Allowing or authorizing others to use one's motor vehicle in a prearranged speed competition causing serious bodily injury or death (offenses committed on or after Dec. 1, 2025)**	G.S. 20-141.3(d)(2)	Permanent; G.S. 20-141.3(d)(2)
	Conditional restoration Authorized: G.S. 20-141.3(d)(2), (d1).		
	After this time period of revocation: 7 years. *Eligibility requirements:* Satisfactory proof that the person has been of good behavior during the revocation period and that the person's conduct and attitude entitle the person to favorable consideration. *Restrictions:* NC DMV may impose terms and conditions for up to 3 years.		
G.S. 20-141.5(a)	**Misdemeanor speeding to elude arrest**	G.S. 20-141.5(d)	≤ 1 year; G.S. 20-141.5(d)
G.S. 20-141.5(b)	**Felony speeding to elude arrest (Class H felony)**	G.S. 20-141.5(d)	2 years if 2 aggravating factors under G.S. 20-141.5(b); 3 years if 3 or more aggravating factors under G.S. 20-141.5(b); G.S. 20-141.5(d)
	Limited driving privilege authorized: G.S. 20-141.5(d).		
	Eligibility requirements: First felony conviction under G.S. 20-141.5 where only 2 aggravating factors present. License or privilege must not be revoked under any other statute. *Duration:* May apply after 12 months of revocation; privilege is valid for period of revocation remaining. *Issuing official:* Sentencing court. *Statutory terms:* G.S. 20-16.1(b). *Restrictions:* Any restrictions the court deems advisable. Can include conditions of days, hours, types of vehicles, routes, geographical boundaries, and specific purposes for which limited driving privilege is allowed. Person must provide proof of financial responsibility and must maintain financial responsibility during the term of the limited driving privilege (or must sign a written certificate indicating that the person (1) does not own a registered vehicle and (2) does not operate any nonfleet private passenger vehicle owned by another that is not covered by commercial-auto liability insurance). *Forms:* AOC-CR-306.		

Reckless Driving and Speeding *(continued)*

Conviction Statute	Offense Description / Triggering Event	Revocation Statute	Length of Revocation; Statute
G.S. 20-141.5(b1)	**Misdemeanor speeding to elude arrest that causes death (Class H felony)**	G.S. 20-141.5(d)	2 years if 2 aggravating factors under G.S. 20-141.5(b); 3 years if 3 or more aggravating factors under G.S. 20-141.5(b); G.S. 20-141.5(d)

Limited driving privilege authorized: G.S. 20-141.5(d).

Eligibility requirements: Must be the person's first felony conviction under G.S. 20-141.5, and only 2 aggravating factors may have been present. License or privilege must not be revoked under any other statute.

Duration: May apply after 12 months of revocation; valid for rest of the revocation period.

Issuing official: Sentencing court.

Statutory terms: G.S. 20-16.1(b).

Restrictions: Any restrictions the court deems advisable. Can include conditions of days, hours, types of vehicles, routes, geographical boundaries, and specific purposes for which limited driving privilege is allowed. Person must provide proof of financial responsibility and must maintain financial responsibility during the term of the limited driving privilege (or must sign a written certificate indicating that the person (1) does not own a registered vehicle and (2) does not operate any nonfleet private passenger vehicle owned by another that is not covered by commercial-auto liability insurance).

Forms: AOC-CR-306.

Conviction Statute	Offense Description / Triggering Event	Revocation Statute	Length of Revocation; Statute
G.S. 20-141.5(b1)	**Felony speeding to elude arrest that causes death (Class E felony)**	G.S. 20-141.5(d)	2 years if 2 aggravating factors under G.S. 20-141.5(b); 3 years if 3 or more aggravating factors under G.S. 20-141.5(b); G.S. 20-141.5(d)

Limited driving privilege authorized: G.S. 20-141.5(d).

Eligibility requirements: Must be the person's first felony conviction under G.S. 20-141.5, and only 2 aggravating factors may have been present. License or privilege must not be revoked under any other statute.

Duration: May apply after 12 months of revocation; valid for rest of the revocation period.

Issuing official: Sentencing court.

Statutory terms: G.S. 20-16.1(b).

Restrictions: Any restrictions the court deems advisable. Can include conditions of days, hours, types of vehicles, routes, geographical boundaries, and specific purposes for which limited driving privilege is allowed. Person must provide proof of financial responsibility and must maintain financial responsibility during the term of the limited driving privilege (or must sign a written certificate indicating that the person (1) does not own a registered vehicle and (2) does not operate any nonfleet private passenger vehicle owned by another that is not covered by commercial-auto liability insurance).

Forms: AOC-CR-306.

Alcohol, Drugs, and Impairment

Conviction Statute	Offense Description / Triggering Event	Revocation Statute	Length of Revocation; Statute
G.S. 18B-111	**Transportation of a non-tax-paid alcoholic beverage**	Discretionary revocation: G.S. 20-16(a)(8)	≤ 6 months; G.S. 20-19(a)
G.S. 18B-302(a1)	**Giving alcoholic beverages to a person under 21**	G.S. 20-17.3	1 year; G.S. 20-17.3

Limited driving privilege authorized: G.S. 20-17.3 (if eligible under G.S. 20-179.3).

Eligibility requirements: (1) At the time of the offense, the person's license was valid or had been expired for less than a year. (2) At the time of the offense, the person had not within the preceding 7 years been convicted of an offense involving impaired driving. (3) Since the offense, the person has not been convicted of an offense involving impaired driving or had an unresolved charge for such an offense. (4) The person is not revoked under any other statute. (5) The person has filed a substance abuse assessment with the court. (6) The person has furnished proof of financial responsibility or has demonstrated that financial-responsibility requirements do not apply.

Duration: Up to 1 year.

Issuing official: Trial judge. If application filed after sentencing and presiding judge is not assigned to court in district, then either the senior resident superior court judge or chief district court judge, depending on whether the conviction was imposed in superior or district court.

Statutory terms: G.S. 20-179.3.

Restrictions: Essential driving for purposes set out in G.S. 20-179.3(a) during standard working hours. Court may authorize driving for work-related and other specified purposes during nonstandard hours. Person may drive for emergency medical care at any time. Person may not drive while any alcohol or controlled substance is in the person's body, unless the controlled substance was lawfully obtained and taken in therapeutically appropriate amounts. If ignition interlock is required, time and purpose restrictions do not apply when the person is operating a designated motor vehicle with a functioning IID. Person must provide proof of financial responsibility and must maintain financial responsibility during the term of the limited driving privilege (or must sign a written certificate indicating that the person (1) does not own a registered vehicle and (2) does not operate any nonfleet private passenger vehicle owned by another that is not covered by commercial-auto liability insurance).

Forms: AOC-CR-312; AOC-CR-340 (IID).

Conviction Statute	Offense Description / Triggering Event	Revocation Statute	Length of Revocation; Statute
G.S. 18B-302(b)	**Underage purchase or attempt to purchase an alcoholic beverage**	G.S. 20-17.3	1 year; G.S. 20-17.3
G.S. 18B-302(c)(1)	**Underage person who aids or abets the gift or purchase of an alcoholic beverage to/by a minor**	G.S. 20-17.3	1 year; G.S. 20-17.3

Limited driving privilege authorized: G.S. 20-17.3 (if eligible under G.S. 20-179.3).

Eligibility requirements: (1) At the time of the offense, the person's license was valid or had been expired for less than a year. (2) At the time of the offense, the person had not within the preceding 7 years been convicted of an offense involving impaired driving. (3) Since the offense, the person has not been convicted of an offense involving impaired driving or had an unresolved charge for such an offense. (4) The person is not revoked under any other statute. (5) The person has obtained and filed with the court a substance-abuse assessment. (6) The person has furnished proof of financial responsibility or has demonstrated that financial-responsibility requirements do not apply.

Duration: Up to 1 year.

Issuing official: Trial judge. If application filed after sentencing and presiding judge is not assigned to court in district, then either the senior resident superior court judge or chief district court judge, depending on whether the conviction was imposed in superior or district court.

Statutory terms: G.S. 20-179.3.

Restrictions: Essential driving for purposes set out in G.S. 20-179.3(a) during standard working hours. Court may authorize driving for work-related and other specified purposes during nonstandard hours. Person may drive for emergency medical care at any time. Person may not drive while any alcohol or controlled substance is in the person's body, unless the controlled substance was lawfully obtained and taken in therapeutically appropriate amounts. If ignition interlock is required, time and purpose restrictions do not apply when the person is operating a designated motor vehicle with a functioning IID. Person must provide proof of financial responsibility and must maintain financial responsibility during the term of the limited driving privilege (or must sign a written certificate indicating that financial responsibility is not required because the person does not own a currently registered motor vehicle and does not operate any nonfleet private passenger motor vehicle owned by another that is not insured under a commercial-auto liability policy).

Forms: AOC-CR-312; AOC-CR-340 (IID).

Note: AC = alcohol concentration. IID = ignition interlock device.

Alcohol, Drugs, and Impairment *(continued)*

Conviction Statute	Offense Description / Triggering Event	Revocation Statute	Length of Revocation; Statute
G.S. 18B-302(c)(2)	**Person over 21 who aids or abets the gift or purchase of an alcoholic beverage to/by a minor**	G.S. 20-17.3	1 year; G.S. 20-17.3
	Limited driving privilege authorized: G.S. 20-17.3 (if eligible under G.S. 20-179.3).		
	Eligibility requirements: (1) At time of the offense, the person's license was valid or had been expired for less than a year. (2) At the time of the offense, the person had not within the preceding 7 years been convicted of an offense involving impaired driving. (3) Since the offense, the person has not been convicted of an offense involving impaired driving or had an unresolved charge for such an offense. (4) The person is not revoked under any other statute. (5) The person has obtained and filed with the court a substance-abuse assessment. (6) The person has furnished proof of financial responsibility or has demonstrated that financial-responsibility requirements do not apply.		
	Duration: Up to 1 year.		
	Issuing official: Trial judge. If application filed after sentencing and presiding judge is not assigned to court in district, then either the senior resident superior court judge or chief district court judge, depending on whether the conviction was imposed in superior or district court.		
	Statutory terms: G.S. 20-179.3.		
	Restrictions: Essential driving for purposes set out in G.S. 20-179.3(a) during standard working hours. Court may authorize driving for work-related and other specified purposes during nonstandard hours. Person may drive for emergency medical care at any time. Person may not drive while any alcohol or controlled substance is in the person's body, unless the controlled substance was lawfully obtained and taken in therapeutically appropriate amounts. If ignition interlock is required, time and purpose restrictions do not apply when the person is operating a designated motor vehicle with a functioning IID. Person must provide proof of financial responsibility and must maintain financial responsibility during the term of the limited driving privilege (or must sign a written certificate indicating that the person (1) does not own a registered vehicle and (2) does not operate any nonfleet private passenger vehicle owned by another that is not covered by commercial-auto liability insurance).		
	Forms: AOC-CR-312; AOC-CR-340 (IID).		
G.S. 18B-302(e)	**Fraudulent use of identification** • to enter or attempt to enter a place where alcohol beverages are sold or consumed • to obtain or attempt to obtain an alcohol beverage • to obtain or attempt to obtain permission to purchase alcohol beverages	G.S. 20-17.3	1 year; G.S. 20-17.3
G.S. 18B-302(f)	**Allowing use of identification by a person who violates or attempts to violate G.S. 18B-302(b)**	G.S. 20-17.3	1 year; G.S. 20-17.3
G.S. 18B-401	**Transportation of an open bottle of fortified wine or spirituous liquor in passenger area**	Discretionary revocation: G.S. 20-16(a)(8)	≤ 6 months; G.S. 20-19(a)
G.S. 18B-406	**Transportation of unauthorized amount of alcoholic beverage**	Discretionary revocation: G.S. 20-16(a)(8)	≤ 6 months; G.S. 20-19(a)
G.S. 20-12.1	**Impaired instruction**	Discretionary revocation: G.S. 20-16(a)(8a)	≤ 1 year; G.S. 20-19(c)

Note: AC = alcohol concentration. IID = ignition interlock device.

Alcohol, Drugs, and Impairment *(continued)*

Conviction Statute	Offense Description / Triggering Event	Revocation Statute	Length of Revocation; Statute
G.S. 20-138.1	**Impaired driving**	G.S. 20-17(a)(2)	1 year; G.S. 20-19(c1)

Limited driving privilege authorized: G.S. 20-179.3.

Eligibility requirements: Category one. (1) At the time of the offense, the person held a valid driver's license or license that had been expired for less than a year. (2) At the time of the offense, the person had not within the previous 7 years been convicted of an offense involving impaired driving. (3) Punishment Level 3, 4, or 5 was imposed. (4) Since the offense, the person has not been convicted of an offense involving impaired driving or had an unresolved charge of such an offense. (5) The person has filed with the court a substance-abuse assessment of the type required by G.S. 20-17.6 for the restoration of a driver's license. Category two, effective December 1, 2024. (1) The person has not been convicted of more than one other offense involving impaired driving within the previous 7 years. (2) At the time of the offense, the person held a valid driver's license or a license that had been expired for less than a year. (3) At the time of the offense, the person did not have an alcohol concentration of 0.15 or more. (4) Punishment Level 3, 4, or 5 was imposed or Punishment Level 2 was imposed based on the grossly aggravating factor of a prior conviction under G.S. 20-179(c)(1). (5) Since the offense, the person has not been convicted of an offense involving impaired driving or had an unresolved charge for such an offense. (6) The person has filed with the court a substance-abuse assessment of the type required by G.S. 20 17.6 for the restoration of a driver's license.

    For both categories, the person must also provide proof of financial responsibility or demonstrate that the financial responsibility requirements do not apply. G.S. 20-179.3(b)(l). The privilege is valid only if the license is revoked solely under G.S. 20-17(a)(2). G.S. 20-179.3(e). If a person is convicted of an offense involving impaired driving and the offense occurs when the person is less than 21 years old, the person's license must be revoked under G.S. 20-13.2 for 1 year in addition to any other revocation required or authorized by law. G.S. 20-13.2(b), (d). Thus, such a person is ineligible for a limited driving privilege because the person is revoked under an additional statutory provision.

Duration: 1 year, but no longer than revocation period *(see* G.S. 20-17.6).

Issuing official: Trial judge. If application filed after sentencing and presiding judge is not assigned to court in district, then either the senior resident superior court judge or chief district court judge, depending on whether the conviction was imposed in superior or district court.

Statutory terms: G.S. 20-179.3.

Restrictions: Essential driving for purposes set out in G.S. 20-179.3(a) during standard working hours. Court may authorize driving for work-related and other specified purposes during nonstandard hours. The person may drive for emergency medical care at any time. The person may not drive while any alcohol or controlled substance is in the person's body, unless the controlled substance was lawfully obtained and taken in therapeutically appropriate amounts. If the person had an alcohol concentration of 0.15 or more, or if a limited driving privilege is issued under category two, the limited driving privilege must require ignition interlock. In all other cases, ignition interlock may be required in the judge's discretion. If ignition interlock is required, time and purpose restrictions do not apply when the person is operating a designated vehicle equipped with a functioning IID. The person must provide proof of financial responsibility and must maintain financial responsibility during the term of the limited driving privilege (or must sign a written certificate indicating that the person (1) does not own a registered vehicle and (2) does not operate any nonfleet private passenger vehicle owned by another that is not covered by commercial-auto liability insurance).

Forms: AOC-CR-312; AOC-CR-340 (IID).

Restrictions on Restored License	Alcohol Concentration (AC) Restriction [Duration]	Ignition Interlock Device (IID) and AC Restriction [Duration]
	0.04 [3 years]	If the person's alcohol concentration is 0.15 or more or if the person is convicted of another impaired driving offense that occurred within 7 years of current offense, IID required with 0.02 AC restriction [1 year]

Note: AC = alcohol concentration. IID = ignition interlock device.

Alcohol, Drugs, and Impairment *(continued)*

Conviction Statute	Offense Description / Triggering Event	Revocation Statute	Length of Revocation; Statute
	Out-of-state or federal driving while impaired (DWI)	G.S. 20-23, -23.2	1 year; G.S. 20-19(c1)

Limited driving privilege authorized: G.S. 20-179.3.

Eligibility requirements: G.S. 20-179.3(b)(1), (3): A person is eligible if he/she would have been eligible had conviction occurred in North Carolina. If the court in the other jurisdiction imposed a term of non-operation, the person must comply for 60 days before applying for a limited privilege. The privilege is only valid if the person is revoked solely under G.S. 20-17(a)(2) or as the result of a conviction in another jurisdiction substantially similar to impaired driving under G.S. 20-138.1. G.S. 20-179.3(e). If a person is convicted of an offense involving impaired driving and the offense occurs when the person is less than 21 years old, the person's license must be revoked under G.S. 20-13.2 for 1 year in addition to any other revocation required or authorized by law. G.S. 20-13.2(b), (d). Thus, such a person is ineligible for a limited driving privilege because the person is revoked under an additional statutory provision.

Duration: Duration of revocation, up to 1 year.

Issuing official: Chief district court judge of district where petitioner lives.

Statutory terms: G.S. 20-179.3.

Restrictions: Essential driving for purposes set out in G.S. 20-179.3(a) during standard working hours. Court may authorize driving for work-related and other specified purposes during nonstandard hours. Person may drive for emergency medical care at any time. Person may not drive while any alcohol or controlled substance is in the person's body, unless the controlled substance was lawfully obtained and taken in therapeutically appropriate amounts. If ignition interlock is required, time and purpose restrictions do not apply when the person is operating a designated motor vehicle with a functioning IID. Person must provide proof of financial responsibility and must maintain financial responsibility during the term of the limited driving privilege (or must sign a written certificate that financial responsibility is not required because the person does not own a currently registered motor vehicle and does not operate any nonfleet private passenger motor vehicle owned by another that is not insured under a commercial-auto liability policy).

Forms: AOC-CV-352A; AOC-CV-352B (IID).

	AC Restriction [Duration]	IID and AC Restriction [Duration]
Restrictions upon Restored License	0.04 [3 years]	If the person is convicted of another impaired driving offense that occurred within seven years of the current offense, IID is required with a 0.02 AC restriction [1 year]

Note: AC = alcohol concentration. IID = ignition interlock device.

Alcohol, Drugs, and Impairment *(continued)*

Conviction Statute	Offense Description / Triggering Event	Revocation Statute	Length of Revocation; Statute
G.S. 20-138.1	**Impaired driving and the person has been convicted of another offense involving impaired driving that occurred within 3 years preceding the current offense**	G.S. 20-17(a)(2)	4 years; G.S. 20-19(d)

Limited driving privilege authorized: G.S. 20-179.3(b)(3) (effective December 1, 2024).

Eligibility requirements: (1) The person has not been convicted of more than one other offense involving impaired driving within the previous 7 years. (2) At the time of the offense, the person held a valid driver's license or a license that had been expired for less than a year. (3) At the time of the offense, the person did not have an alcohol concentration of 0.15 or more. (4) Punishment Level 3, 4, or 5 was imposed or Punishment Level 2 was imposed based on the grossly aggravating factor of a prior conviction under G.S. 20-179(c)(1). (5) Since the offense, the person has not been convicted of an offense involving impaired driving or had an unresolved charge for such an offense. (6) The person has filed with the court a substance abuse assessment of the type required by G.S. 20 17.6 for the restoration of a driver's license.

    The person must also provide proof of financial responsibility or demonstrate that the financial responsibility requirements do not apply. G.S. 20-179.3(l). The privilege is valid only if the license is revoked solely under G.S. 20-17(a)(2). G.S. 20-179.3(e). If a person is convicted of an offense involving impaired driving and the offense occurs when the person is less than 21 years old, the person's license must be revoked under G.S. 20-13.2 for one year in addition to any other revocation required or authorized by law. G.S. 20-13.2(b),(d). Thus, such a person is ineligible for a limited driving privilege because the person is revoked under an additional statutory provision.

Duration: Duration of revocation, but no longer than revocation period (*see* G.S. 20-17.6).

Issuing official: Trial judge. If application filed after sentencing and presiding judge is not assigned to court in district, then either the senior resident superior court judge or chief district court judge, depending on whether the conviction was imposed in superior or district court.

Statutory terms: G.S. 20-179.3.

Restrictions: Ignition interlock required. The person must provide proof of financial responsibility and must maintain financial responsibility during the term of the limited driving privilege (or must sign a written certificate that financial responsibility is not required because the person does not own a currently registered motor vehicle and does not operate any nonfleet private passenger motor vehicle owned by another that is not insured under a commercial motor vehicle liability insurance policy).

Forms: Not yet developed at the time of this publication.

Conditional restoration authorized: G.S. 20-19(d).

After this time period of revocation: 2 years.

Eligibility requirements: Satisfactory proof of the following:
1. During the revocation period, the person has not been convicted of a motor vehicle offense, an alcohol beverage–control law offense, a drug-law offense, or any other criminal offense involving the possession or consumption of alcohol or drugs.
2. The person does not use alcohol or drugs excessively (including prescription drugs) or use any controlled substance unlawfully. The person may submit to continuous alcohol monitoring to prove abstinence from alcohol consumption during a revocation period immediately before restoration is considered. NC DMV must accept monitoring periods of 120 days or longer as evidence of abstinence if it receives sufficient documentation reflecting that the person abstained from alcohol use during monitoring by an approved system.

Restrictions: NC DMV may place reasonable conditions or restrictions on the person for the duration of the original revocation period. Mandatory restrictions are listed below.

Restrictions upon Restored License	AC Restriction [Duration]	IID and AC Restriction [Duration]
	0.02 [3 years]	IID required, 0.02 AC [3 years]

Note: AC = alcohol concentration. IID = ignition interlock device.

Alcohol, Drugs, and Impairment *(continued)*

Conviction Statute	Offense Description / Triggering Event	Revocation Statute	Length of Revocation; Statute
	Out-of-state or federal driving while impaired and the person has been convicted of another offense involving impaired driving that occurred within 3 years preceding the current offense	G.S. 20-23, -23.2	4 years; G.S. 20-19(d)

Limited driving privilege authorized: G.S. 20-179.3(b)(3) (effective December 1, 2024).

Eligibility requirements: G.S. 20-179.3(b)(3): The person is eligible if he/she would have been eligible had the conviction occurred in North Carolina. The privilege is only valid if the person is revoked solely under G.S. 20-17(a)(2) or as the result of a conviction in another jurisdiction substantially similar to impaired driving under G.S. 20-138.1. G.S. 20-179.3(e). If a person is convicted of an offense involving impaired driving and the offense occurs when the person is less than 21 years old, the person's license must be revoked under G.S. 20-13.2 for one year in addition to any other revocation required or authorized by law. G.S. 20-13.2(b),(d). Thus, such a person is ineligible for a limited driving privilege because the person is revoked under an additional statutory provision.

Duration: Duration of revocation.

Issuing official: Chief district court judge of district where petitioner lives.

Statutory terms: G.S. 20-179.3.

Restrictions: Ignition interlock required. The person must provide proof of financial responsibility and must maintain financial responsibility during the term of the limited driving privilege (or must sign a written certificate that financial responsibility is not required because the person does not own a currently registered motor vehicle and does not operate any nonfleet private passenger motor vehicle owned by another that is not insured under a commercial motor vehicle liability insurance policy).

Forms: Not yet developed at the time of this publication.

Conditional restoration authorized: G.S. 20-19(d).

After this time period of revocation: 2 years.

Eligibility requirements: Satisfactory proof of the following:
1. During the revocation period, the person has not been convicted of a motor vehicle offense, an alcohol beverage–control law offense, a drug-law offense, or any other criminal offense involving the possession or consumption of alcohol or drugs.
2. The person does not use alcohol or drugs excessively (including prescription drugs) or use any controlled substance unlawfully. The person may submit to continuous alcohol monitoring to prove abstinence from alcohol consumption during a revocation period immediately before restoration is considered. NC DMV must accept monitoring periods of 120 days or longer as evidence of abstinence if it receives sufficient documentation reflecting that the person abstained from alcohol use during monitoring by an approved system.

Restrictions: NC DMV may place reasonable conditions or restrictions on the person for the duration of the original revocation period. Mandatory restrictions are listed below.

Restrictions upon Restored License	AC Restriction [Duration]	IID and AC Restriction [Duration]
	0.02 [3 years]	IID required, 0.02 AC [3 years]

Note: AC = alcohol concentration. IID = ignition interlock device.

Alcohol, Drugs, and Impairment *(continued)*

Conviction Statute	Offense Description / Triggering Event	Revocation Statute	Length of Revocation; Statute
G.S. 20-138.1	**Impaired driving and the person has 2 or more previous offenses for which he or she has been convicted, 1 of which occurred within the 5 years immediately preceding the date of the current offense**	G.S. 20-17(a)(2)	Permanent; G.S. 20-19(e)

Conditional restoration authorized: G.S. 20-19(e1) (3 years), (e2) (2 years).

After this time period of revocation: 2 years; or after 3 years.

Eligibility requirements (for after 2 years): Satisfactory proof of the following:

1. The person has not consumed any alcohol for the 12 months preceding the restoration while being monitored by an approved continuous alcohol monitoring device.
2. During the revocation period, the person has not been convicted of a motor vehicle offense, an alcohol beverage–control law offense, a drug-law offense, or any other criminal offense involving the possession or consumption of alcohol or drugs.
3. The person does not use drugs excessively (including prescription drugs).
4. The person is not unlawfully using any controlled substance.

Eligibility requirements (for after 3 years):

1. In the 3 years immediately preceding the person's application for a restored license, the person has not been convicted in North Carolina or in any other state or federal court of a motor vehicle offense, an alcohol beverage–control law offense, a drug-law offense, or any criminal offense involving the consumption of alcohol or drugs.
2. The person does not use alcohol or drugs excessively (including prescription drugs) or use any controlled substance unlawfully. The person may submit to continuous alcohol monitoring to prove abstinence from alcohol consumption during a revocation period immediately before restoration is considered. NC DMV must accept monitoring periods of 120 days or longer as evidence of abstinence if it receives sufficient documentation reflecting that the person abstained from alcohol use during monitoring by an approved system.

Restrictions: NC DMV may place reasonable conditions or restrictions on the person for up to 5 years from the date of restoration. Mandatory restrictions are listed below.

Restrictions upon Restored License	AC Restriction [Duration]	IID and AC Restriction [Duration]
	0.00 [7 years]	IID required, 0.02 AC [7 years]

Note: AC = alcohol concentration. IID = ignition interlock device.

Alcohol, Drugs, and Impairment *(continued)*

Conviction Statute	Offense Description / Triggering Event	Revocation Statute	Length of Revocation; Statute
	Out-of-state or federal driving while impaired and the person has 2 or more previous offenses for which he or she has been convicted, 1 of which occurred within the 5 years immediately preceding the date of the current offense	G.S. 20-23, -23.2	Permanent; G.S. 20-19(e)

Limited driving privilege authorized: G.S. 20-179.3(b)(3) (effective December 1, 2024).

Eligibility requirements: G.S. 20-179.3(b)(3): The person is eligible if he/she would have been eligible had the conviction occurred in North Carolina. The privilege is only valid if the person is revoked solely under G.S. 20-17(a)(2) or as the result of a conviction in another jurisdiction substantially similar to impaired driving under G.S. 20-138.1. G.S. 20-179.3(e). If a person is convicted of an offense involving impaired driving and the offense occurs when the person is less than 21 years old, the person's license must be revoked under G.S. 20-13.2 for one year in addition to any other revocation required or authorized by law. G.S. 20-13.2(b),(d). Thus, such a person is ineligible for a limited driving privilege because the person is revoked under an additional statutory provision.

Duration: Duration of revocation.

Issuing official: Chief district court judge of district where petitioner lives.

Statutory terms: G.S. 20-179.3

Restrictions: Ignition interlock required. The person must provide proof of financial responsibility and must maintain financial responsibility during the term of the limited driving privilege (or must sign a written certificate that financial responsibility is not required because the person does not own a currently registered motor vehicle and does not operate any nonfleet private passenger motor vehicle owned by another that is not insured under a commercial motor vehicle liability insurance policy).

Forms: Not yet developed at the time of this publication.

Conditional restoration authorized: G.S. 20-19(e1) (3 years), (e2) (2 years).

After this time period of revocation: 2 years; or after 3 years.

Eligibility requirements (for after 2 years): Satisfactory proof of the following:
1. The person has not consumed any alcohol for the 12 months preceding the restoration while being monitored by an approved continuous alcohol monitoring device.
2. During the revocation period, the person has not been convicted of a motor vehicle offense, an alcohol beverage–control law offense, a drug-law offense, or any other criminal offense involving the possession or consumption of alcohol or drugs.
3. The person does not use drugs excessively (including prescription drugs).
4. The person is not unlawfully using any controlled substance.

Eligibility requirements (for after 3 years):
1. In the 3 years immediately preceding the person's application for a restored license, the person has not been convicted in North Carolina or in any other state or federal court of a motor vehicle offense, an alcohol beverage–control law offense, a drug-law offense, or any criminal offense involving the consumption of alcohol or drugs.
2. The person does not use alcohol or drugs excessively (including prescription drugs) or use any controlled substance unlawfully. The person may submit to continuous alcohol monitoring to prove abstinence from alcohol consumption during a revocation period immediately before restoration is considered. NC DMV must accept monitoring periods of 120 days or longer as evidence of abstinence if it receives sufficient documentation reflecting that the person abstained from alcohol use during monitoring by an approved system.

Restrictions: NC DMV may place reasonable conditions or restrictions on the person for up to 5 years from the date of restoration. Mandatory restrictions are listed below.

Restrictions upon Restored License	AC Restriction [Duration]	IID and AC Restriction [Duration]
	0.00 [7 years]	IID required, 0.02 AC [7 years]

Note: AC = alcohol concentration. IID = ignition interlock device.

Alcohol, Drugs, and Impairment *(continued)*

Conviction Statute	Offense Description / Triggering Event	Revocation Statute	Length of Revocation; Statute
G.S. 20-138.1	**Impaired driving sentenced at Aggravated Level One under G.S. 20-179(f3)**	G.S. 20-17(a)(2)	Permanent; G.S. 20-19(e)

Conditional restoration authorized: G.S. 20-19(e1) (3 years), (e2) (2 years).

After this time period of revocation: 2 years; or after 3 years.

Eligibility requirements (for after 2 years): Satisfactory proof of the following:
1. The person has not consumed any alcohol for the 12 months preceding the restoration while being monitored by an approved continuous alcohol monitoring device.
2. During the revocation period, the person has not been convicted of a motor vehicle offense, an alcohol beverage–control law offense, a drug-law offense, or any other criminal offense involving the possession or consumption of alcohol or drugs.
3. The person does not use drugs excessively (including prescription drugs).
4. The person is not unlawfully using any controlled substance.

Eligibility requirements (for after 3 years):
1. In the 3 years immediately preceding the person's application for a restored license, the person has not been convicted in North Carolina or in any other state or federal court of a motor vehicle offense, an alcohol beverage–control law offense, a drug-law offense, or any criminal offense involving the consumption of alcohol or drugs.
2. The person does not use alcohol or drugs excessively (including prescription drugs) or use any controlled substance unlawfully. The person may submit to continuous alcohol monitoring to prove abstinence from alcohol consumption during a revocation period immediately before restoration is considered. NC DMV must accept monitoring periods of 120 days or longer as evidence of abstinence if it receives sufficient documentation reflecting that the person abstained from alcohol use during monitoring by an approved system.

Restrictions: NC DMV may place reasonable conditions or restrictions on the person for up to 5 years from the date of restoration. Mandatory restrictions are listed below

Restrictions upon Restored License	AC Restriction [Duration]	IID and AC Restriction [Duration]
	0.04 [7 years]	IID required, 0.02 AC [1 year]

Conviction Statute	Offense Description / Triggering Event	Revocation Statute	Length of Revocation; Statute
G.S. 20-138.2	**Driving a commercial vehicle while impaired with alcohol concentration of 0.06 or higher**	G.S. 20-17(a)(2)	1 year; G.S. 20-19(c1)

Restrictions upon Restored License	AC Restriction [Duration]	IID and AC Restriction [Duration]
	0.02 [3 years]	No IID requirement [N/A]

Conviction Statute	Offense Description / Triggering Event	Revocation Statute	Length of Revocation; Statute
G.S. 20-138.2	**Driving a commercial motor vehicle while impaired with alcohol concentration of 0.06 or higher and having been convicted of a previous offense involving impaired driving that occurred within 3 years of the current offense**	G.S. 20-17(a)(2)	4 years; G.S. 20-19(d)

Conditional restoration authorized: G.S. 20-19(d).

After this time period of revocation: 2 years.

Eligibility requirements: Satisfactory proof of the following:
1. During the revocation period, the person has not been convicted of a motor vehicle offense, an alcohol beverage–control law offense, a drug-law offense, or any other criminal offense involving the possession or consumption of alcohol or drugs.
2. The person does not use alcohol or drugs excessively (including prescription drugs) or use any controlled substance unlawfully. The person may submit to continuous alcohol monitoring to prove abstinence from alcohol consumption during a revocation period immediately before restoration is considered. NC DMV must accept monitoring periods of 120 days or longer as evidence of abstinence if it receives sufficient documentation reflecting that the person abstained from alcohol use during monitoring by an approved system.

Restrictions: NC DMV may place reasonable conditions or restrictions on the person for the duration of the original revocation period. Mandatory restrictions are listed below.

Restrictions upon Restored License	AC Restriction [Duration]	IID and AC Restriction [Duration]
	0.00 [3 years]	No IID requirement [N/A]

Note: AC = alcohol concentration. IID = ignition interlock device.

Alcohol, Drugs, and Impairment *(continued)*

Conviction Statute	Offense Description / Triggering Event	Revocation Statute	Length of Revocation; Statute
G.S. 20-138.2	**Driving a commercial motor vehicle while impaired with alcohol concentration of 0.06 or higher and having been convicted of 2 or more previous offenses, 1 of which occurred within 5 years of the current offense**	G.S. 20-17(a)(2)	Permanent; G.S. 20-19(e)

Conditional restoration authorized: G.S. 20-19(e1) (3 years), (e2) (2 years).

After this time period of revocation: 2 years; or after 3 years.

Eligibility requirements (for after 2 years): Satisfactory proof of the following:
1. The person has not consumed any alcohol for the 12 months preceding the restoration while being monitored by an approved continuous alcohol monitoring device.
2. During the revocation period, the person has not been convicted of a motor vehicle offense, an alcohol beverage–control law offense, a drug-law offense, or any other criminal offense involving the possession or consumption of alcohol or drugs.
3. The person does not use drugs excessively (including prescription drugs).
4. The person is not unlawfully using any controlled substance.

Eligibility requirements (for after 3 years):
1. In the 3 years immediately preceding the person's application for a restored license, the person has not been convicted in North Carolina or in any other state or federal court of a motor vehicle offense, an alcohol beverage–control law offense, a drug-law offense, or any criminal offense involving the consumption of alcohol or drugs.
2. The person does not use alcohol or drugs excessively (including prescription drugs) or use any controlled substance unlawfully. The person may submit to continuous alcohol monitoring to prove abstinence from alcohol consumption during a revocation period immediately before restoration is considered. NC DMV must accept monitoring periods of 120 days or longer as evidence of abstinence if it receives sufficient documentation reflecting that the person abstained from alcohol use during monitoring by an approved system.

Restrictions: NC DMV may place reasonable conditions or restrictions on the person for up to 5 years from the date of restoration. Mandatory restrictions are listed below.

Restrictions upon Restored License	AC Restriction [Duration]	IID and AC Restriction [Duration]
	0.00 [7 years]	No IID requirement [N/A]

Conviction Statute	Offense Description / Triggering Event	Revocation Statute	Length of Revocation; Statute
G.S. 20-138.2	**Driving a commercial motor vehicle while impaired with an alcohol concentration of 0.06 or higher sentenced at Aggravated Level One under G.S. 20-179(f3)**	G.S. 20-17(a)(2)	Permanent; G.S. 20-19(e)

Conditional restoration authorized: G.S. 20-19(e1) (3 years), (e2) (2 years).

After this time period of revocation: 2 years; or after 3 years.

Eligibility requirements (for after 2 years): Satisfactory proof of the following:
1. The person has not consumed any alcohol for the 12 months preceding the restoration while being monitored by an approved continuous alcohol monitoring device.
2. During the revocation period, the person has not been convicted of a motor vehicle offense, an alcohol beverage–control law offense, a drug-law offense, or any other criminal offense involving the possession or consumption of alcohol or drugs.
3. The person does not use drugs excessively (including prescription drugs).
4. The person is not unlawfully using any controlled substance.

Eligibility requirements (for after 3 years):
1. In the three years immediately preceding the person's application for a restored license, the person has not been convicted in North Carolina or in any other state or federal court of a motor vehicle offense, an alcohol beverage–control law offense, a drug-law offense, or any criminal offense involving the consumption of alcohol or drugs.
2. The person does not use alcohol or drugs excessively (including prescription drugs) or use any controlled substance unlawfully. The person may submit to continuous alcohol monitoring to prove abstinence from alcohol consumption during a revocation period immediately before restoration is considered. NC DMV must accept monitoring periods of 120 days or longer as evidence of abstinence if it receives sufficient documentation reflecting that the person abstained from alcohol use during monitoring by an approved system.

Restrictions: NC DMV may place reasonable conditions or restrictions on the person for up to 5 years from the date of restoration. Mandatory restrictions are listed below.

Restrictions upon Restored License	AC Restriction [Duration]	IID and AC Restriction [Duration]
	0.00 [7 years]	No IID requirement [N/A]

Note: AC = alcohol concentration. IID = ignition interlock device.

Alcohol, Drugs, and Impairment *(continued)*

Conviction Statute	Offense Description / Triggering Event	Revocation Statute	Length of Revocation; Statute
G.S. 20-138.2A	**Second or subsequent conviction (within 7 years) of driving a commercial vehicle after consuming alcohol**	G.S. 20-17(a)(13)	1 year; G.S. 20-19(f)
G.S. 20-138.2B	**Driving a school bus, school activity bus, child care vehicle, ambulance or other EMS vehicle, firefighting vehicle, or law enforcement vehicle after consuming alcohol**	G.S. 20-17(a)(14)	First conviction: 10 days; subsequent convictions: 1 year; G.S. 20-19(c2)
G.S. 20-138.3	**Driving after consuming alcohol or drugs by a person under 21**	G.S. 20-13.2	1 year; G.S. 20-13.2(d)

Limited driving privilege authorized: G.S. 20-138.3(d).

Eligibility requirements: G.S. 20-138.3(d). Must be 18, 19, or 20 on date of offense. Must not have previous conviction under G.S. 20-138.3. Must meet eligibility requirements of G.S. 20-179.3(b)(1) other than requirements for Punishment Level 3, 4, or 5 and filing substance-abuse assessment.

Duration: Duration of revocation, up to 1 year.

Issuing official: Trial judge. If application filed after sentencing and presiding judge is not assigned to court in district, then either the senior resident superior court judge or chief district court judge, depending on whether the conviction was imposed in superior or district court.

Statutory terms: G.S. 20-179.3.

Restrictions: Essential driving for purposes set out in G.S. 20-179.3(a) during standard working hours. Court may authorize driving for work-related and other specified purposes during nonstandard hours. Person may drive for emergency medical care at any time. Person may not drive while any alcohol or controlled substance is in the person's body, unless the controlled substance was lawfully obtained and taken in therapeutically appropriate amounts. If ignition interlock is required, time and purpose restrictions do not apply when the person is operating a designated motor vehicle with a functioning IID. Person must provide proof of financial responsibility and must maintain financial responsibility during the term of the limited driving privilege (or must sign a written certificate indicating that financial responsibility is not required because the person does not own a currently registered motor vehicle and does not operate any nonfleet private passenger motor vehicle owned by another that is not insured under a commercial-auto liability policy).

Forms: AOC-CR-312; AOC-CR-340 (IID).

Restrictions upon Restored License	AC Restriction [Duration]	IID and AC Restriction [Duration]
	0.00 [Until the person is 21]	No IID requirement [N/A]

G.S. 20-138.5	**Habitual impaired driving**	G.S. 20-138.5(d)	Permanent; G.S. 20-138.5(d)

Conditional restoration authorized: G.S. 20-19(e4).

After this time period of revocation: 10 years following the completion of any sentence imposed by the court.

Eligibility requirements: Satisfactory proof of the following:
1. In the past ten years, the person has not been convicted of a motor vehicle offense, an alcohol beverage–control law offense, a drug-law offense, or any other criminal offense.
2. The person does not drink alcohol, unlawfully use any controlled substance, or use prescription drugs excessively.

Restrictions: NC DMV may place reasonable conditions or restrictions on the person for up to 5 years from the date of restoration. Mandatory restrictions are listed below.

Restrictions upon Restored License	AC Restriction [Duration]	IID and AC Restriction [Duration]
	0.02 [7 years]	IID required; 0.02 AC [7 years]

Note: AC = alcohol concentration. IID = ignition interlock device.

Alcohol, Drugs, and Impairment *(continued)*

Conviction Statute	Offense Description / Triggering Event	Revocation Statute	Length of Revocation; Statute
G.S. 20-138.7	**Second or subsequent conviction of transporting an open container of alcoholic beverage under G.S. 20-138.7**	G.S. 20-17(a)(12)	1 year; G.S. 20-19(f)

Limited driving privilege authorized: G.S. 20-138.7(h).

Eligibility requirements: G.S. 20-138.7(h). Must meet eligibility requirements of G.S. 20-179.3(b)(1) other than requirements for Punishment Level 3, 4, or 5 and obtaining and filing substance-abuse assessment.

Duration: Duration of revocation; up to 1 year.

Issuing official: Trial judge. If application filed after sentencing and presiding judge is not assigned to court in district, then senior resident superior court judge if conviction imposed in superior court or chief district court judge if conviction was imposed in district court.

Statutory terms: G.S. 20-179.3.

Restrictions: Essential driving for purposes set out in G.S. 20-179.3(a) during standard working hours. Court may authorize driving for work-related and other specified purposes during nonstandard hours. Person may drive for emergency medical care at any time. Person may not drive while any alcohol or controlled substance is in the person's body, unless the controlled substance was lawfully obtained and taken in therapeutically appropriate amounts. If ignition interlock is required, time and purpose restrictions do not apply when the person is operating a designated motor vehicle with a functioning IID. Person must provide proof of financial responsibility and must maintain financial responsibility during the term of the limited driving privilege (or must sign a written certificate indicating that financial responsibility is not required because the person does not own a currently registered motor vehicle and does not operate any nonfleet private passenger motor vehicle owned by another that is not insured under a commercial-auto liability policy).

Forms: AOC-CR-312; AOC-CR-340 (IID).

Conviction Statute	Offense Description / Triggering Event	Revocation Statute	Length of Revocation; Statute
G.S. 20-141.4(a1)	**Felony death by vehicle**	G.S. 20-17(a)(9)	Permanent; G.S. 20-19(i)

Conditional restoration authorized: G.S. 20-19(i).

After this time period of revocation: 5 years.

Eligibility requirements: Satisfactory proof of the following:
1. In the 5 years immediately preceding the person's application for a restored license, the person has not been convicted in North Carolina or in any other state or federal court of a motor vehicle offense, an alcohol beverage–control law offense, a drug-law offense, or any criminal offense involving the consumption of alcohol or drugs.
2. The person does not use alcohol or drugs excessively.

Restrictions: NC DMV may place reasonable conditions or restrictions on the person for up to 7 years from the date of restoration. Mandatory restrictions are listed below.

	AC Restriction [Duration]	IID and AC Restriction [Duration]
Restrictions upon Restored License	0.02 [7 years]	IID required, 0.02 AC [7 years], effective December 1, 2024

Conviction Statute	Offense Description / Triggering Event	Revocation Statute	Length of Revocation; Statute
G.S. 20-141.4(a3)	**Felony serious injury by vehicle**	G.S. 20-17(a)(9)	4 years; G.S. 20-19(d)

Conditional restoration authorized: G.S. 20-19(d).

After this time period of revocation: 2 years.

Eligibility requirements: Satisfactory proof of the following:
1. During the revocation period, the person has not been convicted of a motor vehicle offense, an alcohol beverage–control law offense, a drug-law offense, or any other criminal offense involving the possession or consumption of alcohol or drugs.
2. The person does not use alcohol or drugs excessively (including prescription drugs) or use any controlled substance unlawfully. The person may submit to continuous alcohol monitoring to prove abstinence from alcohol consumption during a revocation period immediately before restoration is considered. NC DMV must accept monitoring periods of 120 days or longer as evidence of abstinence if it receives sufficient documentation reflecting that the person abstained from alcohol use during monitoring by an approved system.

Restrictions: NC DMV may place reasonable conditions or restrictions on the person for the duration of the original revocation period. Mandatory restrictions are listed below.

	AC Restriction [Duration]	IID and AC Restriction [Duration]
Restrictions upon Restored License	0.00 [3 years]	IID required, 0.02 AC [3 years], effective December 1, 2024

Note: AC = alcohol concentration. IID = ignition interlock device.

Alcohol, Drugs, and Impairment *(continued)*

Conviction Statute	Offense Description / Triggering Event	Revocation Statute	Length of Revocation; Statute
G.S. 20-141.4(a4)	**Aggravated felony serious injury by vehicle**	G.S. 20-17(a)(9)	Permanent; G.S. 20-19(e)

Conditional restoration authorized: G.S. 20-19(e1) (3 years), (e2) (2 years).

After this time period of revocation: 2 years; or after 3 years.

Eligibility requirements (for after 2 years): Satisfactory proof of the following:
1. The person has not consumed any alcohol for the 12 months preceding the restoration while being monitored by an approved continuous alcohol monitoring device.
2. During the revocation period, the person has not been convicted of a motor vehicle offense, an alcohol beverage–control law offense, a drug-law offense, or any other criminal offense involving the possession or consumption of alcohol or drugs.
3. The person does not use drugs excessively (including prescription drugs).
4. The person is not unlawfully using any controlled substance.

Eligibility requirements (for after 3 years):
1. In the 3 years immediately preceding the person's application for a restored license, the person has not been convicted in North Carolina or in any other state or federal court of a motor vehicle offense, an alcohol beverage–control law offense, a drug-law offense, or any criminal offense involving the consumption of alcohol or drugs.
2. The person does not use alcohol or drugs excessively (including prescription drugs) or use any controlled substance unlawfully. The person may submit to continuous alcohol monitoring to prove abstinence from alcohol consumption during a revocation period immediately before restoration is considered. NC DMV must accept monitoring periods of 120 days or longer as evidence of abstinence if it receives sufficient documentation reflecting that the person abstained from alcohol use during monitoring by an approved system.

Restrictions: NC DMV may place reasonable conditions or restrictions on the person for up to 5 years from the date of restoration. Mandatory restrictions are listed below.

	AC Restriction [Duration]	IID and AC Restriction [Duration]
Restrictions upon Restored License	0.00 [7 years]	IID required, 0.02 AC [7 years], effective December 1, 2024

Conviction Statute	Offense Description / Triggering Event	Revocation Statute	Length of Revocation; Statute
G.S. 20-141.4(a5)	**Aggravated felony death by vehicle**	G.S. 20-17(a)(9)	Permanent; G.S. 20-19(i)

Conditional restoration authorized: G.S. 20-19(i).

After this time period of revocation: 5 years.

Eligibility requirements: Satisfactory proof of the following:
1. In the 5 years immediately preceding the person's application for a restored license, the person has not been convicted in North Carolina or in any other state or federal court of a motor vehicle offense, an alcohol beverage–control law offense, a drug-law offense, or any criminal offense involving the consumption of alcohol or drugs.
2. The person does not use alcohol or drugs excessively.

Restrictions: NC DMV may place reasonable conditions or restrictions on the person for up to 7 years from the date of restoration. Mandatory restrictions are listed below.

	AC Restriction [Duration]	IID and AC Restriction [Duration]
Restrictions upon Restored License for Subsequent Restorations	0.02 [7 years]	IID required, 0.02 AC [7 years], effective December 1, 2024

Note: AC = alcohol concentration. IID = ignition interlock device.

Alcohol, Drugs, and Impairment *(continued)*

Conviction Statute	Offense Description / Triggering Event	Revocation Statute	Length of Revocation; Statute
G.S. 20-141.4(a6)	**Repeat felony death by vehicle**	G.S. 20-17(a)(9)	Permanent; G.S. 20-19(i)

Conditional restoration authorized: G.S. 20-19(i).

After this time period of revocation: 5 years.

Eligibility requirements: Satisfactory proof of the following:
1. In the 5 years immediately preceding the person's application for a restored license, the person has not been convicted in North Carolina or in any other state or federal court of a motor vehicle offense, an alcohol beverage–control law offense, a drug-law offense, or any criminal offense involving the consumption of alcohol or drugs.
2. The person does not use alcohol or drugs excessively.

Restrictions: NC DMV may place reasonable conditions or restrictions on the person for up to 7 years from the date of restoration. Mandatory restrictions are listed below.

	AC Restriction [Duration]	IID and AC Restriction [Duration]
Restrictions upon Restored License	0.02 [7 years]	IID required, 0.02 AC [7 years], effective December 1, 2024

	Refusal to submit to chemical testing	G.S. 20-16.2(d)	12 months

Limited driving privilege authorized: G.S. 20-16.2(e1).

Eligibility requirements: (1) At the time of the refusal, the person's license was valid or had been expired for less than a year. (2) At the time of the refusal, the person had not within the preceding 7 years been convicted of an offense involving impaired driving. (3) At the time of the refusal, the person had not in the preceding 7 years willfully refused to submit to a chemical analysis under G.S. 20-16.2. (4) The implied-consent offense charged did not involve death or critical injury to another person. (5) The underlying charge has been finally disposed of (a) other than by a conviction or (b) by a conviction under G.S. 20-138.1 at Level 3, 4, or 5, and the defendant has complied with at least one of the mandatory probation conditions listed for the punishment level that the person was sentenced under. (6) Since the refusal, the person has had no more convictions for an offense involving impaired driving or any unresolved pending charges for such. (7) The license has been revoked for at least 6 months for the refusal. (8) The person has obtained a substance-abuse assessment from a mental health facility and successfully completed any recommended training or treatment program. (9) The license must be revoked only under G.S. 20-16.2 or under G.S. 20-16.2 and G.S. 20-17(a)(2). If a person willfully refuses to submit to a chemical analysis pursuant to G.S. 20-16.2 while the person is less than 21 years old, the person's license must be revoked under G.S. 20-13.2 for 1 year in addition to any other revocation required or authorized by law. G.S. 20-13.2(c). Thus, such a person is ineligible for a limited driving privilege because the person is revoked under an additional statutory provision.

Duration: Duration of revocation.

Issuing official: Any district court judge authorized to hold court in the district where the license was revoked.

Statutory terms: G.S. 20-179.3.

Restrictions: Essential driving for purposes set out in G.S. 20-179.3(a) during standard working hours. Court may authorize driving for work-related and other specified purposes during nonstandard hours. Person may drive for emergency medical care at any time. Person may not drive while any alcohol or controlled substance is in the person's body, unless the controlled substance was lawfully obtained and taken in therapeutically appropriate amounts. If ignition interlock is required, time and purpose restrictions do not apply when the person is operating a designated motor vehicle with a functioning IID. Person must provide proof of financial responsibility and must maintain financial responsibility during the term of the limited driving privilege (or must sign a written certificate indicating that the person (1) does not own a registered vehicle and (2) does not operate any nonfleet private passenger vehicle owned by another that is not covered by commercial-auto liability insurance).

Forms: AOC-CVR-9 (petition); AOC-CVR-10A; AOC-CVR-10B (IID).

Note: AC = alcohol concentration. IID = ignition interlock device.

Alcohol, Drugs, and Impairment *(continued)*

Conviction Statute	Offense Description / Triggering Event	Revocation Statute	Length of Revocation; Statute
	Civil license revocation for 30 or 45 days	G.S. 20-16.5	30–45 days

Limited driving privilege authorized: G.S. 20-16.5(p).

Eligibility requirements: (1) At the time of the alleged offense, the person's license was valid or had been expired for less than a year. (2) Since the offense, the person has not been convicted of an offense involving impaired driving or had an unresolved charge for such an offense (except the offense for which the license was revoked under G.S. 20-16.5). (3) Person's license has been revoked for at least 10 days (for 30-day revocation) or 30 days (for 45-day revocation). (4) Person has obtained a substance-abuse assessment and registers for and agrees to participate in any recommended training or treatment program. (5) License is revoked solely under G.S. 20-16.5.

Duration: Duration of revocation.

Issuing official: Any district court judge authorized to hold court in the district where the license was revoked.

Statutory terms: G.S. 20-179.3.

Restrictions: Essential driving for purposes set out in G.S. 20-179.3(a) during standard working hours. Court may authorize driving for work-related and other specified purposes during nonstandard hours. Person may drive for emergency medical care at any time. Person may not drive while any alcohol or controlled substance is in the person's body, unless the controlled substance was lawfully obtained and taken in therapeutically appropriate amounts. If ignition interlock is required, time and purpose restrictions do not apply when the person is operating a designated motor vehicle with a functioning IID. Person must provide proof of financial responsibility and must maintain financial responsibility during the term of the limited driving privilege (or must sign a written certificate indicating that financial responsibility is not required because the person does not own a currently registered motor vehicle and does not operate any nonfleet private passenger motor vehicle owned by another that is not insured under a commercial-auto liability policy).

Forms: AOC-CVR-9 (petition); AOC-CVR-10A; AOC-CVR-10B (IID).

	Indefinite civil license revocation based on pending offense	G.S. 20-16.5	At least 30 days and until final judgment has been entered for the current offense and all pending offenses

Limited driving privilege authorized: G.S. 20-16.5(p).

Eligibility requirements: (1) Person's license must have been surrendered for at least 30 days or for 45 days if G.S. 20-16.5(f)(3) applies. (2) Privilege must be necessary to overcome undue hardship. (3) At the time of the offense, the person's license was valid or had been expired for less than one year. (4) At the time of the offense, the person had not within the previous 7 years been convicted of an offense involving impaired driving. (5) Subsequent to the offense, the person has not been convicted of or had an unresolved charge lodged against him or her for an offense involving impaired driving. (6) The person has obtained and filed with the court a substance-abuse assessment.

Duration: Duration of revocation.

Issuing official: A judge of the division in which the current offense is pending.

Statutory terms: G.S. 20-179.3.

Restrictions: Essential driving for purposes in G.S. 20-179.3(a) during standard working hours. Court may authorize driving for work-related and other specified purposes during nonstandard hours. Person may drive for emergency medical care at any time. Person may not drive while any alcohol or controlled substance is in the person's body, unless the controlled substance was lawfully obtained and taken in therapeutically appropriate amounts. If ignition interlock is required, time and purpose restrictions do not apply when the person is operating a designated motor vehicle with a functioning IID. Person must provide proof of financial responsibility and must maintain financial responsibility during the term of the limited driving privilege (or must sign a written certificate indicating that the person (1) does not own a registered vehicle and (2) does not operate any nonfleet private passenger vehicle owned by another that is not covered by commercial-auto liability insurance).

Forms: AOC-CVR-9 (petition); AOC-CVR-10A; AOC-CVR-10B (ID).

Note: AC = alcohol concentration. IID = ignition interlock device.

Death by Vehicle (*Not Otherwise Classified*)

Note: This chart does not include the death by vehicle offenses that include an element of speeding or impairment.

Conviction Statute	Offense Description / Triggering Event	Revocation Statute	Length of Revocation; Statute
Common law	**Involuntary manslaughter resulting from the operation of a motor vehicle**	G.S. 20-17(a)(1)	1 year (if offense did not involve impaired driving); G.S. 20-19(c1); permanent (if offense involved impaired driving); G.S. 20-19(i)

Conditional restoration authorized: G.S. 20-19(i).

After this time period of revocation: 5 years.

Eligibility requirements: Satisfactory proof of the following:
1. In the 5 years immediately preceding the person's application for a restored license, the person has not been convicted in North Carolina or in any other state or federal court of a motor vehicle offense, an alcohol beverage–control law offense, a drug-law offense, or any criminal offense involving the consumption of alcohol or drugs.
2. The person does not use alcohol or drugs excessively.

Restrictions: NC DMV may place reasonable conditions or restrictions on the person for up to 7 years from the date of restoration. Mandatory restrictions are listed below.

Restrictions upon Restored License (if offense involved impaired driving)	AC Restriction [Duration]	IID and AC Restriction [Duration]
	0.02 [7 years]	No IID requirement [N/A]

G.S. 20-141.4	**Misdemeanor death by vehicle**	G.S. 20-17(a)(9)	1 year; G.S. 20-19(f)
G.S. 20-157(i)	**Failure to stop for approaching fire, police, rescue vehicle, etc., or other violation of G.S. 20-157 that causes serious injury or death**	Discretionary revocation: G.S. 20-157(i)	≤ 6 months; G.S. 20-157(i)

Limited driving privilege authorized: G.S. 20-157(i).

Eligibility requirements: License must not be revoked under any other statute.

Duration: Not to exceed revocation period.

Issuing official: Trial judge.

Statutory terms: G.S. 20-16.1(b).

Restrictions: Any restrictions the court deems advisable. Can include conditions of days, hours, types of vehicles, routes, geographical boundaries, and specific purposes for which limited driving privilege is allowed. Person must provide proof of financial responsibility and must maintain financial responsibility during the term of the limited driving privilege (or must sign a written certificate indicating that the person (1) does not own a registered vehicle and (2) does not operate any nonfleet private passenger vehicle owned by another that is not covered by commercial-auto liability insurance).

Forms: AOC-CR-306.

G.S. 20-217(g)	**Passing a stopped school bus and striking a person, causing death (Class H felony)**	G.S. 20-217(g1)	3 years; G.S. 20-217(g1)

Limited driving privilege authorized: G.S. 20-217(g1).

Eligibility requirements: First felony conviction under G.S. 20-217. License may not be revoked under any other statute.

Duration: May be issued after 6 months of revocation; valid for period of revocation remaining.

Issuing official: Trial judge.

Statutory terms: G.S. 20-16.1(b).

Restrictions: Any restrictions the court deems advisable. Can include conditions of days, hours, types of vehicles, routes, geographical boundaries, and specific purposes for which limited driving privilege is allowed. Person must provide proof of financial responsibility and must maintain financial responsibility during the term of the limited driving privilege (or must sign a written certificate indicating that the person (1) does not own a registered vehicle and (2) does not operate any nonfleet private passenger vehicle owned by another that is not covered by commercial-auto liability insurance).

Forms: AOC-CR-306.

G.S. 20-217(g)	**Second conviction of passing a stopped school bus and striking a person and causing death (offenses committed on or after Dec. 1, 2013)**	G.S. 20-217(g1)	Permanent; G.S. 20-217(g1)

Driving While License Revoked

Conviction Statute	Offense Description / Triggering Event	Revocation Statute	Length of Revocation; Statute
G.S. 20-28(a) (2014)	**Driving while license revoked (offenses committed before Dec. 1, 2015)** Note: For offenses committed on or after Dec. 1, 2015, conviction under G.S. 20-28(a) does not trigger an additional revocation period.	G.S. 20-28(a) (2014)	First offense: 1 year; second offense: 2 years; subsequent offenses: permanent; G.S. 20-28(a) (2014)

Limited driving privilege authorized: G.S. 20-20.1.

Eligibility requirements: (1) Person's license is revoked under G.S. 20-28(a) or G.S. 20-28.1. (2) Person has complied with the revocation for the compliance period immediately preceding the date of the petition for a limited driving privilege. If the revocation was for 1 year, the compliance period is 90 days. If the revocation was for 2 years, the compliance period is 1 year. If the revocation was permanent, the compliance period is 2 years. (3) The person's underlying offense does not involve impaired driving. (4) If the person's license is revoked under G.S. 20-28.1 for committing a moving offense while driving with a revoked license, that offense did not involve impaired driving. (5) The revocation period has expired for the offense that the license was revoked for when the person was charged under G.S. 20-28 or for the offense the person was convicted of under G.S. 20-28.1. (6) There is no other revocation in effect. (7) The person is not eligible to receive a limited driving privilege under any other law. (8) The person has not held a limited driving privilege issued under G.S. 20-20.1 at any time during the past three years. (9) In this or any state, the person has no pending charges for any motor vehicle offense and has no unpaid motor vehicle fines or unpaid penalties. (10) No out-of-state licenses have been revoked. (11) NC DMV is not prohibited from issuing a license under G.S. 20-9(e) (a person unable to exercise reasonable and ordinary control over a motor vehicle or a person unable to understand highway warnings or direction signs) or under G.S. 20-9(f) (a person's license or driving privilege is canceled, suspended, or revoked in any jurisdiction for something that would be grounds for cancellation, suspension, or revocation in North Carolina).

Duration: The shorter of 1 year or the length of time remaining in the revocation period imposed under G.S. 20-28(a) or 20-28.1.

Issuing official: District judge in the county of the person's residence.

Statutory terms: G.S. 20-20.1.

Restrictions: Essential driving (1) to and from the person's place of work and in the course of work; (2) for necessary maintenance of the person's household (from 6:00 a.m. to 8:00 p.m., Monday to Friday); and (3) to provide emergency medical care for the person or an immediate family member in the same household. The person may drive for emergency medical care at any time and by any route. The court may authorize work-related driving during standard working hours without restricting it to certain times or routes. If the person is required to drive for essential work-related purposes only during standard working hours, the limited driving privilege must prohibit driving during nonstandard working hours unless the driving is for emergency medical care or for authorized household maintenance. If the person is required to drive during nonstandard working hours for an essential work-related purpose and provides documentation of that fact to the court, the court may authorize driving during those hours for that purpose. A limited driving privilege that authorizes work-related driving during nonstandard working hours must include restrictions on times, routes, and geographic boundaries as specified in G.S. 20-20.1(g). The person may not drive while any alcohol or controlled substance is in the person's body, unless the controlled substance was lawfully obtained and taken in therapeutically appropriate amounts. The person must provide proof of financial responsibility and must maintain financial responsibility during the term of the limited driving privilege.

Forms: AOC-CV-353.

Conditional restoration authorized: G.S. 20-28(c), (c1).

After this time period of revocation:
- If revoked under G.S. 20-28(a1) for 1 year, the person may apply for a license after 90 days.
- If revoked under G.S. 20-28(a3) for 1 year, the person may apply for a license after 1 year.
- If revoked under G.S. 20-28 for 2 years, the person may apply for a license after 1 year.
- If revoked under G.S. 20-28 permanently, the person may apply for a license after 3 years.

Eligibility requirements: NC DMV may conditionally restore an applicant's license under G.S. 20-28(c1) if the person has not been convicted of a moving violation, a violation of the alcohol beverage–control laws, or a violation of the drug laws for conduct that occurred during the revocation period. If, however, the person's license was revoked for (1) a violation of G.S. 20-28(a1) where the person's license was originally revoked for an impaired driving revocation or (2) a violation of 20-28(a3), additional requirements apply. In those circumstances, the driver must have obtained a substance-abuse assessment and must complete any education or treatment recommended within time limits specified by NC DMV. If the assessment determined that the person abuses alcohol, the person must use an IID when driving any vehicle during the period of conditional restoration.

Restrictions: NC DMV may impose any appropriate restrictions or conditions on the conditionally restored license for the balance of the revocation period. When the revocation period is permanent, the restrictions and conditions may not exceed 3 years.

Driving While License Revoked *(continued)*

Conviction Statute	Offense Description / Triggering Event	Revocation Statute	Length of Revocation; Statute
G.S. 20-28(a1)	**Driving while license revoked for impaired driving**	G.S. 20-28(a1)	First offense: 1 year; second offense: 2 years; subsequent offenses: permanent; G.S. 20-28(a1)

Conditional restoration authorized: G.S. 20-28(c), (c1).

After this time period of revocation:
- If revoked under G.S. 20-28(a1) for 1 year, the person may apply for a license after 90 days.
- If revoked under G.S. 20-28(a3) for 1 year, the person may apply for a license after 1 year.
- If revoked under G.S. 20-28 for 2 years, the person may apply for a license after 1 year.
- If revoked under G.S. 20-28 permanently, the person may apply for a license after 3 years.

Eligibility requirements: NC DMV may conditionally restore an applicant's license under G.S. 20-28(c1) if the person has not been convicted of a moving violation, a violation of the alcohol beverage–control laws, or a violation of the drug laws for conduct that occurred during the revocation period. If, however, the person's license was revoked for (1) a violation of G.S. 20-28(a1) where the person's license was originally revoked for an impaired driving revocation or (2) a violation of 20-28(a3), additional requirements apply. In those circumstances, the driver must have obtained a substance-abuse assessment and must complete any education or treatment recommended within time limits specified by NC DMV. If the assessment determined that the person abuses alcohol, the person must use an IID when driving any vehicle during the period of conditional restoration.

Restrictions: NC DMV may impose any appropriate restrictions or conditions on the conditionally restored license for the balance of the revocation period. When the revocation period is permanent, the restrictions and conditions may not exceed 3 years.

Conviction Statute	Offense Description / Triggering Event	Revocation Statute	Length of Revocation; Statute
G.S. 20-28(a2) (2014)	**Driving after notification or failure to appear (offenses committed before Dec. 1, 2015)** Note: This provision was recodified for offenses committed on or after Dec. 1, 2015. Thus, only persons convicted under this provision for offenses committed before Dec. 1, 2015, are subject to license revocation.	G.S. 20-28(a2) (2014)	First offense: 1 year; second offense: 2 years; subsequent offenses: permanent; G.S. 20-28(a2) (2014)
G.S. 20-28(a3)	**Driving after notification or failure to appear**	G.S. 20-28(a3)	First offense: 1 year; second offense: 2 years; subsequent offenses: permanent; G.S. 20-28(a3)

Conditional restoration authorized: G.S. 20-28(c), (c1).

After this time period of revocation:
- If revoked under G.S. 20-28(a1) for 1 year, the person may apply for a license after 90 days.
- If revoked under G.S. 20-28(a3) for 1 year, the person may apply for a license after 1 year.
- If revoked under G.S. 20-28 for 2 years, the person may apply for a license after 1 year.
- If revoked under G.S. 20-28 permanently, the person may apply for a license after 3 years.

Eligibility requirements: NC DMV may conditionally restore an applicant's license under G.S. 20-28(c1) if the person has not been convicted of a moving violation, a violation of the alcohol beverage–control laws, or a violation of the drug laws for conduct that occurred during the revocation period. If, however, the person's license was revoked for (1) a violation of G.S. 20-28(a1) where the person's license was originally revoked for an impaired driving revocation, or (2) a violation of 20-28(a3), additional requirements apply. In those circumstances, the driver must have obtained a substance-abuse assessment and must complete any education or treatment recommended within time limits specified by NC DMV. If the assessment determined that the person abuses alcohol, the person must use an IID when driving any vehicle during the period of conditional restoration.

Restrictions: NC DMV may impose any appropriate restrictions or conditions on the conditionally restored license for the balance of the revocation period. When the revocation period is permanent, the restrictions and conditions may not exceed 3 years.

Driving While License Revoked *(continued)*

Conviction Statute	Offense Description / Triggering Event	Revocation Statute	Length of Revocation; Statute
G.S. 20-28(d)	**Driving a commercial motor vehicle during disqualification**	G.S. 20-28(d) provides for an additional disqualification period—not revocation of a regular license; surrender of Class C license is not required; G.S. 20-24(a)	
G.S. 20-28.1	**Moving violation while license revoked**	G.S. 20-28.1	First revocation: 1 year; second revocation: 2 years; subsequent revocations: permanent; G.S. 20-28.1(b)

Conditional restoration authorized: G.S. 20-28.1(c).

After this time period of revocation:
- If revoked for 1 year, the person may apply after 90 days.
- If revoked for 2 years, the person may apply after 12 months.
- If permanently revoked, the person may apply after 3 years.

Eligibility requirements: NC DMV may conditionally restore the person's license upon satisfactory proof that the person has not been convicted of a moving violation, a violation of the alcohol beverage–control laws, or a violation of the drug laws for conduct that occurred during the revocation period.

Restrictions: NC DMV may impose any appropriate restrictions for the balance of the revocation period. When the revocation period is permanent, the restrictions and conditions may not exceed 3 years.

Other

Conviction Statute	Offense Description/Triggering Event	Revocation Statute	Length of Revocation; Statute
G.S. 14-31	**Secret assault with a deadly weapon using a motor vehicle**	G.S. 20-17(a)(11)	1 year; G.S. 20-19(f)
G.S. 14-32(a)	**Assault with a deadly weapon with intent to kill, inflicting serious injury using a motor vehicle**	G.S. 20-17(a)(11)	1 year; G.S. 20-19(f)
G.S. 14-32(b)	**Assault with a deadly weapon, inflicting serious injury using a motor vehicle**	G.S. 20-17(a)(11)	1 year; G.S. 20-19(f)
G.S. 14-32(c)	**Assault with a deadly weapon with intent to kill using a motor vehicle**	G.S. 20-17(a)(11)	1 year; G.S. 20-19(f)
G.S. 14-32.1(e)(1)	**Assault with a deadly weapon on a handicapped person using a motor vehicle**	G.S. 20-17(a)(11)	1 year; G.S. 20-19(f)
G.S. 14-33(c)(1)	**Assault with a deadly weapon using a motor vehicle**	G.S. 20-17(a)(11)	1 year; G.S. 20-19(f)
G.S. 14-49(b), (b1)	**Malicious use of an explosive device to damage property**	G.S. 20-17(a)(15), -13.2(c2) (applicable to persons under 18)	1 year; G.S. 20-19(f), -13.2(d)
G.S. 14-69.1(c)	**False report of a bomb in a public building**	G.S. 20-17(a)(15), -13.2(c2) (applicable to persons under 18)	1 year; G.S. 20-19(f), -13.2(d)
G.S. 14-69.2(c)	**Perpetrating a hoax concerning a bomb in a public building**	G.S. 20-17(a)(15), -13.2(c2) (applicable to persons under 18)	1 year; G.S. 20-19(f), -13.2(d) (applicable to persons under 18)

Other *(continued)*

Conviction Statute	Offense Description / Triggering Event	Revocation Statute	Length of Revocation; Statute
G.S. 14-72.5	**Second or subsequent conviction (within 7 years) of larceny of motor fuel**	G.S. 20-17(a)(16)	Second conviction: 90 days; subsequent conviction: 6 months; G.S. 20-19(g2)

Limited driving privilege authorized: G.S. 20-16(e2).

Eligibility requirements: N/A.

Duration: Not to exceed revocation period.

Issuing official: Trial judge.

Statutory terms: G.S. 20-16.1(b).

Restrictions: Any restrictions the court deems advisable. Can include conditions of days, hours, types of vehicles, routes, geographical boundaries, and specific purposes for which limited driving privilege is allowed. Person must provide proof of financial responsibility and must maintain financial responsibility during the term of the limited driving privilege (or must sign a written certificate indicating that the person (1) does not own a registered vehicle and (2) does not operate any nonfleet private passenger vehicle owned by another that is not covered by commercial-auto liability insurance).

Forms: AOC-CR-306.

Conviction Statute	Offense Description / Triggering Event	Revocation Statute	Length of Revocation; Statute
G.S. 14-269.2(b1)	**Possessing an explosive on educational property**	G.S. 20-17(a)(15), -13.2(c2) (applicable to persons under 18)	1 year; G.S. 20-19(f), -13.2(d)
G.S. 14-269.2(c1)	**Causing a minor to possess an explosive on educational property**	G.S. 20-17(a)(15), -13.2(c2) (applicable to persons under 18)	1 year; G.S. 20-19(f), -13.2(d)
G.S. 20-30(1)	**Displaying or possessing any license or learner's permit known to be invalid**	Discretionary revocation: G.S. 20-16(a)(6)	≤ 1 year; G.S. 20-19(c)
G.S. 20-30(2)	**Counterfeiting, selling, lending, or knowingly permitting the use of any driver's license or learner's permit by one not entitled thereto**	Discretionary revocation: G.S. 20-16(a)(6)	≤ 1 year; G.S. 20-19(c)
G.S. 20-30(3)	**Displaying or representing as one's own a license not issued to the person displaying it**	Discretionary revocation: G.S. 20-16(a)(6)	≤ 1 year; G.S. 20-19(c)
G.S. 20-30(5)	**Using or allowing others to use false names and addresses in license applications and renewals**	G.S. 20-17(a)(8)	1 year; G.S. 20-19(f)
G.S. 20-30(5)	**Making false statements, concealing material facts, or otherwise committing a fraud in applying for a license or permit**	G.S. 20-17(a)(8)	1 year; G.S. 20-19(f)
G.S. 20-31	**Making a false affidavit or knowingly swearing or affirming falsely to any matter or thing required to be sworn to by statute**	G.S. 20-17(a)(5), -17(a)(8)	1 year; G.S. 20-19(f)
G.S. 20-136	**Unlawful possession of a motor vehicle with smoke screens**	G.S. 20-17(a)(3)	1 year; G.S. 20-19(f)
G.S. 20-154(a2)	**Unsafe movement resulting in a crash causing property damage of more than $5,000 or serious bodily injury to a motorcycle operator or passenger**	Discretionary revocation: G.S. 20-154(a2) (discretion of trial court)	≤ 30 days; G.S. 20-154(a2)

Limited driving privilege authorized: G.S. 20-154(a2).

Eligibility requirements: N/A.

Duration: Not to exceed revocation period.

Issuing official: Trial judge.

Statutory terms: G.S. 20-16.1(b).

Restrictions: Any restrictions the court deems advisable. Can include conditions of days, hours, types of vehicles, routes, geographical boundaries, and specific purposes for which limited driving privilege is allowed. Person must provide proof of financial responsibility and must maintain financial responsibility during the term of the limited driving privilege (or must sign a written certificate indicating that the person (1) does not own a registered vehicle and (2) does not operate any nonfleet private passenger vehicle owned by another that is not covered by commercial-auto liability insurance).

Forms: AOC-CR-306.

Other *(continued)*

Conviction Statute	Offense Description / Triggering Event	Revocation Statute	Length of Revocation; Statute
G.S. 20-160.1	**Failure to yield resulting in serious bodily injury**	G.S. 20-160.1	90 days; G.S. 20-160.1(a)
G.S. 20-166(a), (a1)	**Failure to stop or remain with vehicle involved in injury crash (offenses committed before Dec. 1, 2025)**	G.S. 20-17(a)(4) (applicable to convictions for failure to stop under G.S. 20-166(a)); G.S. 20-166(e) (applicable to convictions under G.S. 20-166(a) or (a1))	1 year, unless court finds that a longer period is appropriate, in which case, 2 years; G.S. 20-166(e)

Limited driving privilege authorized: G.S. 20-166(e) (only convictions under G.S. 20-166(a1)).

Eligibility requirements: (1) First conviction under G.S. 20-166(a1). (2) At the time of the forfeiture, the person's license was valid or had been expired for less than 1 year. (3) Either the person is supporting dependents and requires a driver's license to be gainfully employed or the person has a dependent who requires serious medical treatment and the defendant is the only person able to transport the dependent to the health care facility where the dependent can receive the needed treatment.

Duration: Not to exceed revocation period.

Issuing official: Trial judge. If application filed after sentencing and presiding judge is not assigned to court in district, then either the senior resident superior court judge or chief district court judge, depending on whether the conviction was imposed in superior or district court.

Statutory terms: G.S. 20-179.3(b)(2).

Restrictions: Essential driving related either to gainful employment or necessary medical treatment for a dependent, depending on qualifying factor for privilege eligibility pursuant to G.S. 20-179.3(b)(2).

Forms: AOC-CR-318.

G.S. 20-166(a)	**Failure to stop or remain with vehicle involved in crash resulting in serious bodily injury (offenses committed on or after Dec. 1, 2025)**	G.S. 20-166(e)(1)	4 years; G.S. 20-166(e)(1)

Conditional restoration authorized: G.S. 20-166(e)(1), (e1).

After this time period of revocation: 3 years.

Eligibility requirements: Satisfactory proof that the person has been of good behavior during the revocation period and that the person's conduct and attitude entitle the person to favorable consideration.

Restrictions: NC DMV may impose terms and conditions for the remainder of the original revocation period.

G.S. 20-166(a)	**Failure to stop or remain with vehicle involved in crash resulting in death (offenses committed on or after Dec. 1, 2025)**	G.S. 20-166(e)(2)	Permanent; G.S. 20-166(e)(2)

Conditional restoration authorized: G.S. 20-166(e)(2), (e1).

After this time period of revocation: 7 years.

Eligibility requirements: Satisfactory proof that the person has been of good behavior during the revocation period and that the person's conduct and attitude entitle the person to favorable consideration.

Restrictions: NC DMV may impose terms and conditions for up to 3 years.

Other *(continued)*

Conviction Statute	Offense Description / Triggering Event	Revocation Statute	Length of Revocation; Statute
G.S. 20-166(a1)	**Failure to stop or remain with vehicle involved in crash resulting in injury (offenses committed on or after Dec. 1, 2025)**	G.S. 20-166(e)(3)	1 year, unless court finds that a longer period is appropriate, in which case, 2 years; G.S. 20-166(e)(3)

Limited driving privilege authorized: G.S. 20-166(e)(3).

Eligibility requirements: (1) First conviction under G.S. 20-166(a1) or (b). (2) At the time of the conviction, the person's license was valid or had been expired for less than 1 year. (3) Either the person is supporting dependents and requires a driver's license to be gainfully employed or the person has a dependent who requires serious medical treatment and the defendant is the only person able to transport the dependent to the health care facility where the dependent can receive the needed treatment.

Duration: Not to exceed revocation period.

Issuing official: Trial judge. If application filed after sentencing and presiding judge is not assigned to court in district, then either the senior resident superior court judge or chief district court judge, depending on whether the conviction was imposed in superior or district court.

Statutory terms: G.S. 20-179.3(b)(2).

Restrictions: Essential driving related either to gainful employment or necessary medical treatment for a dependent, depending on qualifying factor for privilege eligibility pursuant to G.S. 20-179.3(b)(2).

Forms: AOC-CR-318.

Conditional restoration authorized: G.S. 20-166(e)(3), (e1).

After this time period of revocation: 1 year.

Eligibility requirements: Satisfactory proof that the person has been of good behavior during the revocation period and that the person's conduct and attitude entitle the person to favorable consideration.

Restrictions: NC DMV may impose terms and conditions for the remainder of the original revocation period.

Conviction Statute	Offense Description / Triggering Event	Revocation Statute	Length of Revocation; Statute
G.S. 20-166(b)	**Failure to render aid to a person injured in a crash (offenses committed before Dec. 1, 2025)**	G.S. 20-17(a)(4)	1 year; G.S. 20-19(f)
G.S. 20-166(b)	**Failure to stop, provide information, or render reasonable assistance to a person injured in a crash (offenses committed on or after Dec. 1, 2025)**	G.S. 20-166(e)(3)	1 year, unless court finds that a longer period is appropriate, in which case, 2 years; G.S. 20-166(e)(3)

Limited driving privilege authorized: G.S. 20-166(e)(3).

Eligibility requirements: (1) First conviction under G.S. 20-166(a1) or (b). (2) At the time of the conviction, the person's license was valid or had been expired for less than 1 year. (3) Either the person is supporting dependents and requires a driver's license to be gainfully employed or the person has a dependent who requires serious medical treatment and the defendant is the only person able to transport the dependent to the health care facility where the dependent can receive the needed treatment.

Duration: Not to exceed revocation period.

Issuing official: Trial judge. If application filed after sentencing and presiding judge is not assigned to court in district, then either the senior resident superior court judge or chief district court judge, depending on whether the conviction was imposed in superior or district court.

Statutory terms: G.S. 20-179.3(b)(2).

Restrictions: Essential driving related either to gainful employment or necessary medical treatment for a dependent, depending on qualifying factor for privilege eligibility pursuant to G.S. 20-179.3(b)(2).

Forms: AOC-CR-318.

Conditional restoration authorized: G.S. 20-166(e)(3), (e1).

After this time period of revocation: 1 year.

Eligibility requirements: Satisfactory proof that the person has been of good behavior during the revocation period and that the person's conduct and attitude entitle the person to favorable consideration.

Restrictions: NC DMV may impose terms and conditions for the remainder of the original revocation period.

Other *(continued)*

Conviction Statute	Offense Description / Triggering Event	Revocation Statute	Length of Revocation; Statute
G.S. 20-217(a)	**Second conviction in 3 years of misdemeanor violation of G.S. 20-217 (passing stopped school bus) (offenses committed on or after Dec. 1, 2013)**	G.S. 20-217(g1)	1 year; G.S. 20-217(g1)
G.S. 20-217(a)	**Third conviction of misdemeanor violation of G.S. 20-217 (passing stopped school bus) (offenses committed on or after Dec. 1, 2013)**	G.S. 20-217(g1)	Permanent; G.S. 20-217(g1)
	Conditional restoration authorized: G.S. 20-217(g1). *After this time period of revocation:* 2 years. *Eligibility requirements:* Satisfactory proof that the person has not been convicted of a moving violation under G.S. Chapter 20 or the laws of another state. *Restrictions:* NC DMV may place appropriate conditions or restrictions on the new driver's license for up to 2 years from the date of restoration.		
G.S. 20-217(g)	**Passing stopped school bus and striking person (Class I felony) (offenses committed on or after Dec. 1, 2013)**	G.S. 20-217(g1)	2 years; G.S. 20-217(g1)
	Limited driving privilege authorized: G.S. 20-217(g1). *Eligibility requirements:* First felony conviction under G.S. 20-217. License may not be revoked under any other statute. *Duration:* May be issued after 6 months of revocation; valid for period of revocation remaining. *Issuing official:* Trial judge. *Statutory terms:* G.S. 20-16.1(b). *Restrictions:* Any restrictions the court deems advisable. Can include conditions of days, hours, types of vehicles, routes, geographical boundaries, and specific purposes for which limited driving privilege is allowed. Person must provide proof of financial responsibility and must maintain financial responsibility during the term of the limited driving privilege (or must sign a written certificate indicating that the person (1) does not own a registered vehicle and (2) does not operate any nonfleet private passenger vehicle owned by another that is not covered by commercial-auto liability insurance). *Forms:* AOC-CR-306.		
G.S. 20-217(g)	**Second conviction within any period of time of passing stopped school bus and striking person (Class I felony) (offenses committed on or after Dec. 1, 2013)**	G.S. 20-217(g1)	Permanent; G.S. 20-217(g1)
	Conditional restoration authorized: G.S. 20-217(g1). *After this time period of revocation:* 3 years. *Eligibility requirements:* Satisfactory proof that the former licensee has not been convicted of a moving violation under G.S. Chapter 20 or the laws of another state. *Restrictions:* NC DMV may place appropriate conditions or restrictions on the new driver's license for up to 3 years from the date of restoration.		
G.S. 20-309(a3)	**Operating a motor vehicle without required premium surcharge when subject to an inexperienced operator premium surcharge pursuant to G.S. 58-36-65(k) (offenses committed on or after July 1, 2026)**	Discretionary revocation; G.S. 20-16(a)(6a)	≤ 1 year; G.S. 20-19(c)
	Provisional licensee convicted of second motor vehicle moving violation within 12 months of date of first offense	Discretionary revocation; G.S. 20-13(b)(2)	Up to 30 days; G.S. 20-13(b)(2)
	Provisional licensee convicted of third motor vehicle moving violation within 12 months of date of first offense	Discretionary revocation; G.S. 20-13(b)(3)	Up to 90 days; G.S. 20-13(b)(3)
	Provisional licensee convicted of fourth motor vehicle moving violation within 12 months of date of first offense	Discretionary revocation; G.S. 20-13(b)(4)	Up to 6 months; G.S. 20-13(b)(4)

Other *(continued)*

Conviction Statute	Offense Description / Triggering Event	Revocation Statute	Length of Revocation; Statute
	Notification from a school authority that a person no longer meets the requirements for a driving eligibility certificate under G.S. 20-11(n)	G.S. 20-13.2(c1)	If the person is ineligible under G.S. 20-11(n)(1), the revocation endures until the person reaches the age of 18; G.S. 20-13.2(c1)(1); if the person is ineligible under G.S. 20-11(n1), then the revocation period is 1 year; G.S. 20-13.2(c1)(2); the person's license must be restored before end of revocation period if qualifying documentation is submitted to NC DMV; G.S. 20-13.2(c1)
	Provisional licensee charged with criminal moving violation	G.S. 20-13.3	30 days
	Accumulation of twelve or more driver's license points within a three-year period or accumulation of eight or more points in the three-year period following reinstatement of a license revoked for conviction of one or more traffic offenses	Discretionary revocation; G.S. 20-16(a)(5)	Up to 60 days for first suspension; up to 6 months for second suspension; up to 1 year for any subsequent suspension; G.S. 20-16(c)
	Failure to appear for motor vehicle offense	G.S. 20-24.1	Until the person disposes of charge or demonstrates that the person who was charged is someone else
	Failure to pay fine, penalty, or costs for motor vehicle offense	G.S. 20-24.1	Until the person pays the penalty, fine, or costs or demonstrates that their failure to pay was not willful, that they are making a good-faith effort to pay, or that the amounts should be remitted

Limited driving privilege authorized: G.S. 20-24.1(f).

Eligibility requirements: License is revoked under G.S. 20-24.1(a)(2) only. No limited privilege under this subsection may have been granted within 3 years of application.

Duration: Up to one year or until any fine, penalty, or court costs ordered by the court are paid.

Issuing official: A judge of the division in which the current offense is pending.

Statutory terms: G.S. 20-16.1.

Restrictions: Any restrictions the court deems advisable. Can include conditions of days, hours, types of vehicles, routes, geographical boundaries, and specific purposes for which limited driving privilege is allowed. Person must provide proof of financial responsibility and must maintain financial responsibility during the term of the limited driving privilege (or must sign a written certificate indicating that the person (1) does not own a registered vehicle and (2) does not operate any nonfleet private passenger vehicle owned by another that is not covered by commercial-auto liability insurance).

Conviction Statute	Offense Description / Triggering Event	Revocation Statute	Length of Revocation; Statute
	N.C. license holder's failure to comply with a citation issued by a state that is a member of the nonresident violator compact	G.S. 20-4.20(b)	Until the person has furnished satisfactory evidence to NC DMV that they have complied with the citation; G.S. 20-4.20(b)

Other *(continued)*

Conviction Statute	Offense Description / Triggering Event	Revocation Statute	Length of Revocation; Statute
	Failure to pay child support or comply with subpoena in child support case	G.S. 110-142.2	Until payments are not delinquent, the person has complied with subpoena, or the person is no longer subject to subpoena

Limited driving privilege authorized: G.S. 110-142.2(c).

Eligibility requirements: License to operate motor vehicle must be necessary to the person's livelihood. The person's license must not be revoked for any other reason.

Duration: Duration of revocation.

Issuing official: Court that issues revocation order upon finding that the person has willfully failed to comply with child support order or subpoena.

Statutory terms: G.S. 110-142.2(c); may be modified or revoked pursuant to G.S. 20-179.3(i).

Restrictions: Terms and conditions prescribed by the court.

Conviction Statute	Offense Description / Triggering Event	Revocation Statute	Length of Revocation; Statute
	Revocation of probation imposed in felony case based on failure to make reasonable efforts to comply with probation	G.S. 15A-1331.1(b)(2)	Full term of probation

Limited driving privilege authorized: G.S. 15A-1331.1(d); 20-179.3(b)(2).

Eligibility requirements: (1) At the time of the forfeiture, the person's license was valid or had been expired for less than 1 year and (2) the person is supporting dependents or requires a driver's license to be gainfully employed or (3) the person has a dependent who requires serious medical treatment, and no one else can provide transportation for that treatment.

Duration: Duration of revocation.

Issuing official: The judge who revokes the defendant's probation.

Statutory terms: G.S. 20-179.3(b)(2).

Restrictions: Essential driving related to either gainful employment or a dependent's medical treatment. The person may not drive while any alcohol or controlled substance is in the person's body, unless the controlled substance was lawfully obtained and taken in therapeutically appropriate amounts. If ignition interlock is required, time and purpose restrictions do not apply when the person is operating a designated motor vehicle with a functioning IID. The person must provide proof of financial responsibility and must maintain financial responsibility during the term of the limited driving privilege (or must sign a written certificate indicating that the person (1) does not own a registered vehicle and (2) does not operate any nonfleet private passenger vehicle owned by another that is not covered by commercial-auto liability insurance).

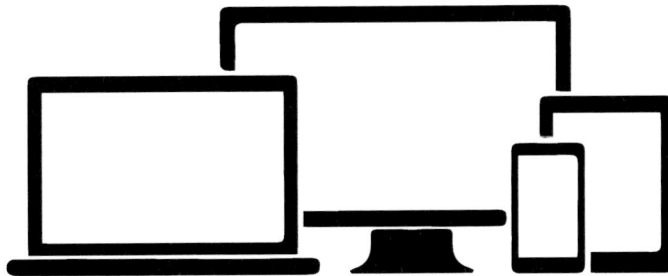

Complimentary access to an online version of this content is included with the purchase of this paperback.
Visit **books.sog.unc.edu/redeem** and (1) create an account or log into your existing account and (2) use the following access code:

DLRR1344-2FBTQ5W5XR

For assistance, contact **helpdesk@sog.unc.edu**

About this Publication

There are more than 8 million licensed drivers in North Carolina, and there are more than 1 million people whose licenses have been revoked by the North Carolina Division of Motor Vehicles (NC DMV). A small number of those people (around 6,000) have been issued a limited driving privilege by the courts that authorizes driving during the period of revocation, subject to certain limitations. Someone whose license has been revoked may have the license reinstated at the end of the revocation period, but in certain circumstances, restrictions are placed on the reinstated license. More than 100,000 drivers licensed by NC DMV have alcohol restrictions on their licenses, and more than 30,000 are permitted to drive only a vehicle equipped with an ignition interlock device.

This publication lists triggering events and convictions that may result in the revocation of a driver's license. For each event, it also covers how long the license can be revoked, whether a limited driving privilege may issue, the limitations of any such privilege, and the mandatory conditions that apply when the license is restored.

About the Authors

Shea Riggsbee Denning is the director of the North Carolina Judicial College and an expert on motor vehicle law and criminal law and procedure. As a School of Government faculty member, she teaches and advises judges, magistrates, prosecutors, defense attorneys, and law enforcement officers.

Belal Elrahal is an assistant professor of public law and government at the School of Government. His work focuses primarily on motor vehicle and impaired driving law, as well as on criminal proceedings before North Carolina magistrates.

Related Publications

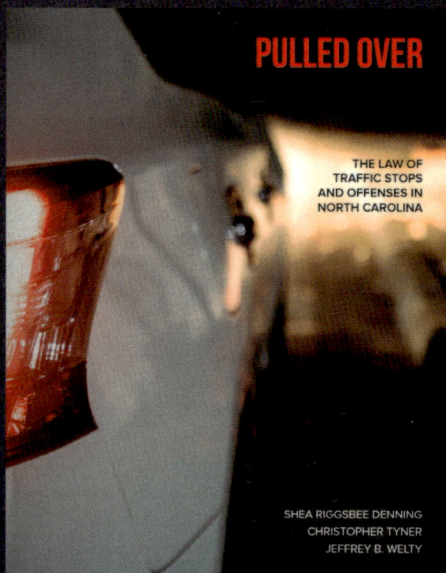

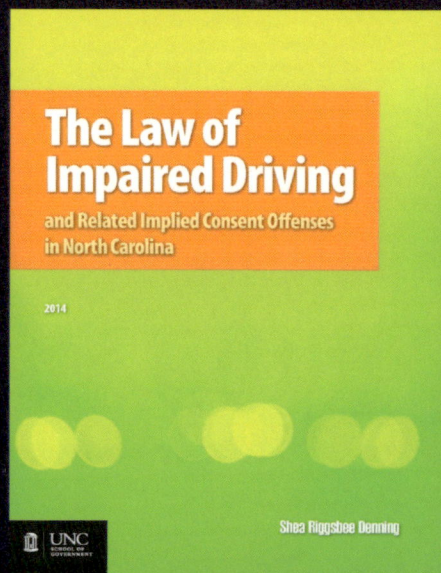

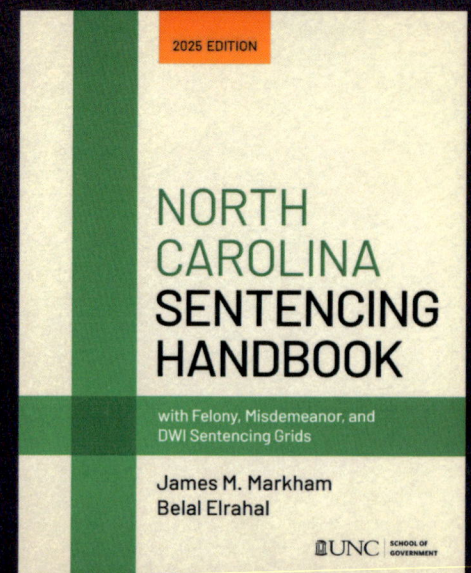

PULLED OVER
THE LAW OF TRAFFIC STOPS AND OFFENSES IN NORTH CAROLINA
SHEA RIGGSBEE DENNING
CHRISTOPHER TYNER
JEFFREY B. WELTY

The Law of Impaired Driving
and Related Implied Consent Offenses in North Carolina
2014
UNC SCHOOL OF GOVERNMENT
Shea Riggsbee Denning

2025 EDITION
NORTH CAROLINA SENTENCING HANDBOOK
with Felony, Misdemeanor, and DWI Sentencing Grids
James M. Markham
Belal Elrahal
UNC SCHOOL OF GOVERNMENT

Distributed by UNC Press

ISBN-13: 978-1-64238-133-7

9 781642 381337

publications.sog.unc.edu

IET Standards

Code of Practice
for Low and Extra Low Voltage
Direct Current Power
Distribution in Buildings